HOW TO BE PRESENT
AT THE END OF YOUR
LOVED ONE'S JOURNEY

PATTY ROTHWELL

Patty loves to hear from fans! Reach out to her at p.rothwell.author@gmail.com

ISBN (Paperback): 979-8-9929574-0-2
ISBN (Ebook): 979-8-9929574-1-9

Contents

A Note from the Author

My original goal with this book was to comfort people with life-limiting illnesses and their loved ones at the end of their journeys. As I wrote, my goal expanded. I want to help readers at any stage of life prepare for the inevitable in their own lives. Perhaps by demystifying the process and learning how we die, we will live our lives more fully.

I encourage you to take care of decisions and all other practical aspects of dying now, so that when your time comes, you have the freedom to concentrate on what matters to you most, whatever that may be.

My wish is for everyone to go through this journey with as much love, comfort, and dignity as possible. I wish for those of us left behind to find solace, knowing we did what we could to ease this transition. From facing this ultimate challenge, I wish us all to receive the reward of a fuller heart.

For further support, I have provided a resource section in the back of the book. It contains links to forms, worksheets, and websites with more information. Throughout the book, you will see boxes that identify these extra resources. I encourage you to check them out and hope they will help you on your journey.

Thank you for reading this book. I hope it provides guidance, wisdom, and comfort to you.

—Patty

P.S. Use the QR code below to download a link to **Five Ways to Support A Loved One at the End of Life, Even If You're Not Their Caregiver**, and **The Ultimate Caregiver's Self-Evaluation Checklist : Take Care of Your Wellbeing While Caring for Others**

Disclaimer

This book is provided as a public service, offering information, insights, and guidance based on the author's research and experiences. It is intended for general informational purposes only and should not be interpreted as medical, legal, or professional advice. The contents of this book are not a substitute for consulting with qualified professionals in their respective fields.

Readers are encouraged to seek the advice of licensed health care providers, legal experts, or other qualified professionals for concerns specific to their individual circumstances. The author and publisher disclaim any liability arising directly or indirectly from the use of the information provided in this book. Readers assume full responsibility for their actions and decisions.

PART 1

RELUCTANT COMPASSION

*Twenty years from now you will be more disappointed
by the things that you didn't do than by the ones you did do.*

—Mark Twain

Chapter 1
How to Do the Uncomfortable

Your loved one is dying. Now what?

When your loved one is dying, one day can be completely different from the next.

Take it one day—even one hour—at a time.

Yet questions remain.

What do you do in these days and hours?

How do you handle what is coming?

To find our way forward, we can look to our past. We may find lessons we did not realize were there—lessons we were not ready to see. When I learned the news that my mom was dying, I remembered what I learned from my dad's death, my grandparents' deaths, and the deaths of other loved ones in my life. I used the lessons I learned in my past to help my mom through her dying process. Now, I have written this book to share these lessons with you.

Growing up in Alaska, I had always been very close to my dad. He built runways for the Air Force, working on remote sites for several months at a time. He would come back home for a few weeks, or a couple of months at most, while the next site was prepped. During those times, everything was perfect. We would go ice skating or do homework together. We would watch a TV show or read to each other before bed. Every once in a while, Mom and

Dad would go out for dinner and dancing—and I never saw Mom happier. Mom and Dad were home every day when my brother Andy and I returned from school. On an annual vacation each fall, they would take us out of school for a month-long road trip from Alaska to Washington, California, Wyoming, and Colorado to visit family. Always an adventure, always fun.

Whenever we took Dad to the base for a Military Air Transport flight to the next job, I would cry so hard that I would throw up. I was ten years old when he left for his final flight before retirement. This time, the only relief from my anguish was knowing this was the last time we would be separated. But his jobs could be dangerous. What if this was the time he did not come home?

In the week while we waited for Dad to close this final job, we sold our home in Anchorage and stayed with family in Seattle. We were so excited about our move to Northern California, where Dad was buying a small garage and a nearby motel with a restaurant. I imagined our new life. We would start every day having breakfast together. Andy and I would stop by Dad's garage on the way home from school to say hello. Mom would always be home, ready to get us started on homework. We would always be together for dinner, when we would plan our weekend outings. We would go camping and exploring, or Mom and Dad would come to our sports events. Dad always said he wanted the kind of semi-retirement where he could hang a "Gone Fishing" sign on the door at any time, grab Mom and us, and do just that. The picture of the future was perfect, until it wasn't.

While playing in my grandparents' backyard, I saw the McCord Air Force staff car pull into the driveway. Two uniformed officers got out and came up the walk. My dad was not in the military—he was a civil engineer on the bases. There was only one reason those officers were here. At that moment, I realized we had already said our last goodbye.

On his final day of work before retirement, my dad was killed in an accident on the job. I was racing towards fear and grief at breakneck speeds. But the most painful feeling of all was regret. I was not there with him. I did not get to see his eyes, hold his hand, or assure him we would be okay. I would never know if he was scared. I regretted not being able to convince him to stop going to jobs out of town. And I felt awful for making it so hard for him to leave, seeing me so upset. I regretted thinking he would always be there. I grieved the loss of future memories that died with him. It was a lot for a ten-year-old to think about. As childhood, adolescence, and young adulthood took their natural course, these once all-consuming feelings sat quietly in the background, for the most part.

As my life unfolded, I had several experiences with the deaths of loved ones. Some had long, terminal illnesses; some died quickly after becoming sick. Some were unexpected end-of-life events. My grandfather died at home of cancer. Months before he died, he "took to his bed." Family would visit and check on my grandmother, arriving and departing quietly. Visitors spoke in hushed tones, as if they were sitting vigil. Very few went in to see him because they "didn't want to disturb him." Life had left "Pappy" long before he died. Grandma died at home in a similar fashion.

Later on, in the seventies, I worked as a ward clerk on the cancer and geriatrics ward at a large hospital in Seattle, Washington. Patients in the ward found themselves in an unfamiliar environment, with limited chances to visit family, and little say in their care options. It was heart wrenching to witness. Working in the ward, I felt like I was watching circumstances unfold that would create the same regrets I had when my dad, grandparents, and John, our close family friend, died. I watched families miss opportunities to be present physically or emotionally with their dying loved ones. They missed chances to express gratitude, appreciation, and love, to recall life before, and to share life now. They missed the gift of saying goodbye.

Then, my mom became ill.

My first thoughts were my regrets as a ten-year-old and memories of my dad's death. My mind jumped to my experiences as a young woman with my grandparents' deaths. I remembered the suffering and isolation I witnessed as a ward clerk at the hospital in Seattle.

I found an inner resolve: this was not going to be the way my mom's life ended.

When I looked at my mom, I did not want to see fear or loneliness. I wanted her to know her life was valued, she was leaving a legacy, and she would not die alone. I wanted to create more memories of special moments while we could. These moments would have to last me a lifetime. But how?

In a perfect world, friends, family, neighbors, co-workers, and community members would show up to comfort our dying loved one. They would recall celebrations, happy times, tender moments, heartbreak, and triumphs over challenges. There would be laughing and crying, quiet times, companionship, and a comforting hand to hold. There could be forgiveness, reconciliation, and expressions of appreciation for what they brought to life. There would be support and love. There would be closure—a loving goodbye.

The reality is, many end-of-life journeys do not look like this. When we do not know how to say what needs to be said, and when that last chance to say goodbye is gone, we can be left with regret that can last a lifetime.

To protect our loved ones and our own hearts, we can learn how to be part of healthy, loving, dignified end-of-life journeys. But how do we get past the initial shock and sadness, so that we can be there for our loved one?

CHAPTER 2

GETTING PAST "I DON'T THINK I CAN DO THIS."

As you face the reality that your loved one is dying, you may feel overwhelmed. You might say to yourself, "I don't think I can do this."

Yes, you can.

You may have a reason to be present for the final chapter of this person's life. Maybe this is why you picked up this book. A five-minute phone call might fulfill this reason, or you might dedicate yourself to them through the end. No judgments here—only you know what you need and what you can do.

This book is not about guilting you into doing anything. It provides perspective to help you make informed decisions. It gives you tools to do what you may not think you can do. It is about not missing the chance for that last goodbye.

Some thoughts stay with you and cause pain throughout your life, so it is healthy to protect yourself by learning how to handle these difficult times with grace and without fear.

"Why didn't I make just one call . . ."

"I could have stopped by for just a minute . . ."

"I thought we had more time . . ."

An infinite number of mindsets, emotions, and experiences can keep us from being present in our loved one's last chapter. If we can identify and get past what is holding us back, the rewards can be immeasurable: the peace of knowing we did all we wanted to do, said all we wanted to say, and provided the comfort we had within us.

Are any of these obstacles keeping you from being present with your dying loved one?

Emotional Discomfort

- **Fear of our own Mortality**: When we are with someone who is dying, we face the fact that our own death is inevitable, and we have a natural fear of the unknown.

- **Fear of Loss**: Facing a loved one's mortality is painful. Some people avoid spending time with a terminally ill person because they are afraid to feel loss and grief.

- **Estranged Relationship**: Family members or friends who have a strained or distant relationship find it difficult to enter into this last chapter of their life.

- **Helplessness**: Seeing suffering and decline can bring up feelings of helplessness. Some people will not visit because they feel unable to change the situation. This can lead to feelings of guilt.

Fear of Saying or Doing the Wrong Thing

- **Lack of Preparedness**: Some people worry about saying the wrong thing. They may avoid connecting to keep from unintentionally hurting their loved one.

- **Navigating Conversations**: Talking about illness, death, and emotions is difficult. Fear of awkward conversations leads some to stay away.

Self-Protection Mechanisms

- **Avoiding Pain**: Being with a loved one while they go through such a hard time is emotionally draining. Some stay away to protect their own wellbeing.

- **Anticipatory Grief**: People experience grief even before the actual loss. Being close to their loved one through their dying process intensifies this anticipatory grief.

Practical Challenges and Responsibilities

- **Time Constraints**: Balancing work, family, and other responsibilities can be overwhelming. Some people struggle to find time to visit.

- **Emotional Fatigue**: Continuous caregiving can lead to emotional exhaustion. Family members may need breaks to recharge.

Denial and Coping Mechanisms

- **Denial of Severity**: Some deny the severity of the illness, distancing themselves from the painful reality: "I thought we had more time."

- **Coping Strategies**: Everyone copes differently. Some choose to focus on positive memories and avoid witnessing the decline: "I want to remember them the way they were before the illness."

Conflict or Unresolved Issues

- **Past Conflicts**: Unresolved interpersonal conflicts can keep people from reaching out to their loved one during this precious time of last opportunities.

Everyone's response to their loved one dying is unique. It is important not to judge how someone reacts to this new reality. Throughout this difficult time, you can expect to experience some of the challenges identified here, as well as others. But there are ways to support yourself and other people in your life.

Conversations with family or friends sharing this loss can be comforting. This gives everyone a chance to talk about the emotions you might have in common. Not everyone has a family or friend support group nearby. Talking to a counselor to work through these obstacles can also be very helpful. Visit chapter 20 for more information about coping skills and resources.

Sometimes the best medicine is a kind heart and a listening ear.
—Unknown

Spending time with terminally ill loved ones is profoundly meaningful, both for the person nearing the end of their life and for those choosing to be present in this last chapter. You can find ways to accept and move through your feelings to make a difference in their life and yours.

CHAPTER 3
THE DIFFERENCE YOU CAN MAKE

At a time when you may feel helpless, keep in mind that even simple steps can provide immense comfort and closure for both you and your dying loved one. Understanding what you can do to make a difference can ease your mind.

Consider the following ways you can help:

Emotional Comfort and Connection

- **Presence**: Being there physically can provide comfort and reassurance. Even if your loved one is unresponsive or asleep, your quiet companionship matters. They can sense your presence and feel less alone.

- **Simple Gestures**: A smile, holding their hand, gentle massage, reading aloud, or sharing memories can evoke positive emotions.

- **Redirecting Focus**: There will be times your loved one will want a break from discussions about their illness. Follow their lead. Instead of dwelling on prognosis or illness, initiate conversations about other topics. Ask about a happy event they look forward to, like the birth of a grandchild, a wedding, or a special visitor on their way. Bring a favorite movie, or one they want to see, and watch it with them. Help them live outside the shadow of this new reality, if even for a few minutes at a time.

Closure and Meaning

- **Important Conversations**: Visits offer opportunities to share feelings and memories, and to say goodbyes. These precious moments cannot always be in person, but this does not diminish the comfort of video calls, phone calls, emails, letters, or cards.

- **Memorable Moments**: Even brief visits make a meaningful impact, whether just chatting for a few minutes, or sharing a meal. Sometimes the best gift is a listening ear. Allow the person to share their thoughts, fears, and hopes. Validate their feelings without judgment.

- **Genuine Interaction**: Keep visits genuine—be true to yourself and authentic to your loved one. It is okay to say, "I don't know what to say, but I care about you." Be attentive. Avoid excessive conversation. Sometimes silence speaks louder than words.

Support for Family Caregivers

- **Supporting the Team**: Caring for seriously ill loved ones is isolating and exhausting. Your visits allow family caregivers to take breaks and recharge. This shows the caregiver they are not going through this alone.

Quality of Life

- **Independence**: Interacting with others allows your loved one to see their identity as an individual, distinct from "patient," or "terminally ill person," regardless of their new limitations.

To Wrap It Up: Reluctance often stems from fear: fear of the unknown, of unintentionally hurting someone you love, or not knowing what to do or say. You can overcome these fears with insight and knowledge. Making peace with your fears helps you have compassion for yourself and your loved one.

As you learn how your presence can have a profound effect on your loved one, the first question might be "What can I do?" To answer this question, consider the role you play in your loved one's life. Reflect on who you are, and who you want to be, as you enter this new chapter.

When we face the ultimate loss, we can lose our view of ourselves, and who we need to be. How do we find that person?

PART 2

EVERYONE PLAYS A PART

All the world's a stage,
And all the men and women merely players;
They have their exits and their entrances,
And one man in his time plays many parts . . .

—William Shakespeare

CHAPTER 4
IN THEIR EYES: WHO WE ARE

C oming out of the surgical suite after my mom's lung biopsy, the doctor's face said it all. His words were "It was what we expected. I'll see your mom when she wakes up. Set up an appointment with my office for the day after tomorrow."

In my mind, until he actually said, "She has lung cancer, there's no hope, nothing can be done, time is short," I had been allowing myself to stay in the comfortable role of a confident, supportive daughter capable of finding solutions to any of Mom's problems.

This abruptly changed during the office visit, when the conversation was only about life expectancy and treatment protocols for pain management. As I sat next to her, holding her hand, for those brief moments, I realized my new role was not to fix, but to face the challenges and find comfort together. A partnership.

The doctor told Mom she should expect to have her mind racing when she was not in a complete fog, at least for the next few days. He asked her to stop at the desk and make a few appointments for various things while he answered my questions. That was somewhat of a ruse, since we had already established that I was Mom's health care agent as well as executrix, he wanted to give me some advice.

Though they had discussed life expectancy in terms of six months, he told me I had three to six weeks to get her input about putting her affairs and final wishes in order. After that, I should expect her health to decline. He explained Mom would probably make some unusual requests this weekend. His last piece of advice was to go with it—do whatever she asked.

With this news came new roles. I became liaison to my siblings, the rest of the family, Mom's friends, and her health care team. I became Mom's immediate physical and emotional support, as well as her financial and estate manager. These roles continued to expand—all built on the underpinnings of the new role, grieving daughter. I felt lost.

If you are sitting where I was, I understand the confusion you may be going through, trying to find yourself in the midst of it all. You may be thinking about your own mortality as well. I want to help you identify where you are, in all of this.

Throughout the life of a relationship, people evolve through many roles. What starts out as an acquaintance, neighbor, or co-worker could become boss, friend, close friend, mentor, teacher, confidant, and so on. Dynamics change within family structures, sometimes subtly, sometimes abruptly. Squabbling siblings become staunch supporters, children become their parents' caregivers, and sometimes family members or friends become estranged. The news that someone is dying impacts each of these relationships—whether new, longstanding, or strained. You will take on a new role in your relationship with the person dying, and this role will continue to evolve. As you begin to understand your new role, you may discover that your loved one views your relationship differently than you do.

The news of someone dying can bring new depths to relationships. Here are two examples, where each dying person receives support from people they did not know they impacted so deeply.

William's boss, who dropped by with a book he thought William would enjoy, had just a handful of conversations with William the entire time they worked together. When he arrived to drop off the book, he told William how much he appreciated him and always enjoyed his humor. He told William he would be missed.

Keith's neighbor noticed the usually well-trimmed lawn needed mowing, so he took care of it. When he finished, he stopped in and asked Keith to let him know if he needed anything. He told Keith he'd be back next week.

Neither William nor Keith felt there was anything more than a passing acquaintance as a relationship with their benefactors. Neither thought these people were even aware of their health issues. The book or the lawn work were not grandiose overtures, but the kindness of these gestures moved both William and Keith in their final chapter of life.

This is also a time you and your loved one can share interesting stories and forgotten history. Together, you can uncover gems.

Kevin's dad George had complications from a surgery to remove a prostate tumor, leaving him in a coma. Kevin would visit his father in the hospital every afternoon. Shortly after George was admitted, Kevin noticed a gentleman who would come in about the same time every day and sit outside George's room. After a week, Kevin asked the gentleman if he was there visiting someone. The gentleman said he heard George was in the hospital and just wanted to keep him company. When Kevin asked how he knew George, the gentleman told a story no one in the family had heard.

Years ago, George had hired this gentleman at a time when, hard as he tried, he could not get a job. Years later, after George had moved on to another job, he ran into his old employee. George learned the gentleman was about to be evicted from his apartment, so he stepped in and paid his rent every month until his wages increased enough to pay it himself. This took a while.

When George came out of his coma, his memory was temporarily affected. When it finally came back, George could not recall who the gentleman could have been. A few years later when George passed, the gentleman stepped to the mic at George's celebration of life and shared this story, and how a simple act of decency to "an old employee," had profoundly changed the direction of his life.

If you are not a close family member, spouse, or caregiver, your entrance into this chapter of your friend's life may come later, and your exit may be sooner. For any amount of time you are there, your presence can comfort your friend and their family during this challenging time. The support you offer in the moment can give you all solace and memories that last a lifetime.

It is important to remember this is not a contest. There are no prizes for spending the most time with the person leaving this world. The amount of time someone spends with their dying loved one is not an indicator of who loves them the most, or who sacrificed the most. The goal is to make the time you have as good as it can be. This will mean different things at different stages.

Before you enter this chapter of your friend's life, their immediate family often has had some time for the shock to subside. Hopefully, they will come to instinctively know where their loved one is mentally, emotionally, and physically each day. If you are not the primary caregiver, there is a delayed adjustment period when it is important to read the room. Just like we all have good days and bad days, your loved one will have extreme versions of this, both physically and emotionally. Be sensitive to this and take cues from them and their caregiver. This can make the difference between a good visit and a not-so-good experience.

While your loved one is still physically active, enjoy this time as much as possible. Do as many activities as possible that you did together before the diagnosis. When necessary, suggest alternatives. If you used to golf together, maybe just do the driving range. If you enjoyed going to the movies but staying up late is too exhausting, go to a matinee.

Consider their interests and hobbies in terms of decreasing levels of ability. If they were an avid gardener but can no longer get up and down, bring them a small planter and a few plants for them to put together and enjoy. Ask around your circle if anyone has a spare planter or basket. If not, you can usually find these items at a donation center. If your loved one is unable to walk around their garden, take pictures of what they enjoyed nurturing. As their abilities decrease, their isolation increases. It is important to remember you can still bring life to them.

My father-in-law Jack was an avid golfer. When he was not on the course, he was watching other golfers tee-off right outside his living room window. Jack's health began to decline from kidney failure and cancer. After Jack had been unable to golf for a while, his golf buddy George came over after a Sunday morning 18-hole round. Jack used the Titleist brand of golf ball, and George used the Callaway brand. George walked over to him, took a Titleist ball out of his pocket, and handed it to him. He told Jack he had taken that ball out as his partner on the 18 he just played, and "It didn't do half bad." Jack got a huge grin on his face. It might have made him sad to be reminded of another thing he could not do anymore. But it didn't.

Our loved ones do not need reminders. It is their reality—they live it every minute. It does not protect them to shield them from activities they can no longer physically participate in—it isolates them. More pain comes from not being part of life while they are alive. You can help by finding creative ways to include them and connect them to the activities they love.

CHAPTER 5
CREATING MOMENTS THAT MATTER

Have the conversations and do the activities that will bring you both comfort when you remember them.

Here are a few ideas:

- Recall the people, places, and events that filled your early days together and strengthened your bond.

- Share memories of your favorite restaurants, movies, and foods. Reminisce about the favorite events you shared, and the least favorite events. Talk about favorite books, inside jokes, and live entertainment you enjoyed together. When possible, revisit some of these venues.

- Encourage them to talk about how their life unfolded, what they think were the best parts, how they got through the hardest parts, or an adventure they have not thought about in years. Talk about things they wished they had done, or done more of, and try to make some version of these things happen. For example, they cannot raft the Colorado river, but there are many GoPro videos on YouTube of rafting trips down the Colorado River. Watching them together can put you two right there.

How long would you remember their smile if you reinvented a dream trip to France, to see the painters along the Seine and picnic along the river outside Paris? Instead of traveling overseas, you can create a local version of this experience. You can visit a gallery in town and picnic on a blanket by a river or park, with French bread, cheese, fruit, wine, and fine chocolates. If going to a park is not easy for your loved one, you can picnic on your living room floor with French sidewalk café music in the background and pictures of France streaming on the TV.

- Revisit their photo collections with them. You can offer to help create smaller photo albums for each of their kids, grandkids, or siblings.

- Suggest starting a project where you can help them record stories from their life for their family to have as keepsakes. MemLife and Legacy Stories both offer services to help with those endeavors.

- Ask how their day is going. Share how your day is going. Talk about what is going on in your common world, such as people you both know, and recent or upcoming events.

- Create new routines. Designate a day and time each week to get together to do something fun. This gives you both something to look forward to every week. You can play a favorite game, give your loved one a manicure, enjoy a movie night, stop for a treat on the way home from doctor's appointments, or just take a short walk to get fresh air.

It is very important to be honest with yourself before going far into this journey with your loved one. It is okay to acknowledge if you are unable to be a strong shoulder to carry their burdens. It is okay to not engage in deep discussions about fear, sadness, and pain. Check in with yourself before taking on roles you may not be able to handle, to protect yourself from trauma and to protect your loved one from feeling abandoned when it gets near the end.

Being honest and vulnerable with your loved one is important for you both to stay connected and to prevent feelings of isolation. What they are going through is a stage of life. They are still alive, and they deserve to share their emotions. They also deserve the honor of you sharing your emotions with them, even if you are feeling scared, worried, sad, or lost. You might think "staying strong," and not showing emotions is healthier for you both than sharing how you really feel. Yet avoiding emotional discussions can lead to separation between you and your loved one. Sharing your emotions with your loved one invites them to share their feelings with you. This can create a connection that brings comfort and closeness, as you unite to support each other.

Yet many people are not comfortable discussing feelings or personal issues. Your loved one may be even more uncomfortable becoming the center of attention because of their diagnosis. Attempting to force conversations about topics they are not comfortable with can leave you both feeling alienated. Check in with your loved one and pay close attention to their cues. Always respect them and their wishes.

Losing their independence and autonomy is demoralizing, especially if they pride themselves on self-reliance. If you feel it is right for both of you, encourage them to talk about their new limitations, their frustrations, and their feelings, with no judgments. You will see this many times in this book because it bears repeating: terminal illness is isolating and painfully lonely.

You can help your loved one both practically and emotionally by stepping up to assist with their daily tasks that may grow difficult for them to manage. By helping them with practical matters, you will maintain a regular presence in their life that can stave off feelings of isolation and loneliness. Keep in mind, sensitivity and communication are essential to keeping your relationship healthy in this challenging time when complex emotions may arise.

CHAPTER 6
HANDS-ON PRACTICAL HELP

L ife is complicated, busy, and stressful! Adding new routines like doctor's appointments, medication schedules, and treatment days can become overwhelming for a healthy person, let alone someone exhausted from fighting illness. This is where you, as their caretaker or helping hand, can be especially supportive.

Motivation is the heart of the matter. Your motivation to help your loved one will usually come through loud and clear, and this will influence whether they accept your offers as supportive gestures, or if they perceive them as something less altruistic. The key is to know why you are doing what you are doing. There are those with good intentions, who swoop in to save the day—taking charge, making decisions, proceeding with plans, and inserting themselves into conversations—all in the name of being helpful. But if they never had this role with their loved one before, and if their loved one did not ask them to assume this role, their efforts might feel intrusive to their loved one. Are they feeding their own ego by pushing their way up the hierarchy of the caregivers? Are they trying to ingratiate themselves with their loved one or family?

Some people just have pushy personalities and big hearts. If you have the tendency to be assertive, consider if you are stepping on someone else's toes, or if you are unintentionally taking away your loved one's autonomy. Observing and communicating are key. If you are motivated by the heart and not the ego, this will usually come through. Once they see you genuinely want to help, they will probably be more willing to ask for assistance.

In the beginning of their diagnosis, they are still independent, but they will need help with basic tasks, just to make life a bit easier. They may be so inundated with the details of this new reality, they cannot identify specifics. If you just say, "Let me know if I can do anything for you," it puts the burden on them. You may never hear from them. I know many people who would automatically respond, "No thank you, I'm fine." Usually, this is not a pride issue. It is the desire to not impose, inconvenience, or take advantage.

With my loved ones whom I cared for during their dying process, I was often able to reach my goal—to make their life just a little easier—by offering in a way that made it clear there would be no imposition. I would say, "I'd like to [insert helpful task here] . . . is that all right?" Framing the question this way helped, rather than "Would you like me to . . .?" I found that saying, "I'm stopping for something for dinner on my way over to visit, can I pick something up for you?" was accepted more readily than "Would you like me to stop at the store for you?" Keeping the tone casual can help your loved one relax and receive support without feeling like a burden.

As their condition declines, a primary caregiver steps in to provide more physical support. This person is often a family member. At this stage, you can help the caregiver as they provide services to your loved one. A live-in caregiver will come to a point where they will be exhausted from attending to needs around the clock. Offering to stay overnight gives the caregiver some time to themselves to recuperate.

After Dad died, Mom's entire world revolved around her family. She had two adult children from her first marriage with their own families. She now cared for my brother Andy and me as a single parent. She also had three siblings and aging parents of her own. That was it. Few friends, social interactions, no outside activities, or interests—nothing. Besides her children, her passion was her home. She kept it immaculate. She manicured her yard continuously, making it the envy of the neighborhood. Mom and I had a close bond. I lived at home with her, and we had coffee or a meal together every day until I married and moved to my first home with my husband, Greg. After Greg and I had our son Jamie, Mom babysat him for a few hours every day. This helped Greg and I when our work schedules overlapped. After work, I would head to Mom's to pick Jamie up and visit with her for a while. When Greg and I decided to move to Alaska, a three-and-a-half hour plane trip away, Mom and I both knew it would be impossible to say goodbye—so we never did. I worked for an airline with generous travel privileges and was able to visit every weekend. A visit back to Mom's would end with me saying, "I'll call when I get home, see you Saturday, love you," as if I were driving twenty minutes down the road instead of flying fifteen hundred air miles across the country. For a while, I kept to a schedule of visiting every weekend. It became normal to be in two places at once.

Over time, visits pared down to every three or four weeks. Rarely, a couple of months would go by between trips. Mom and I were each other's primary emotional and logistical support, no matter where I lived. I was Mom's executrix and had legal and medical Power of Attorney (POA). These roles did not make me feel any more responsible, they just gave me the tools to take care of whatever Mom wanted or needed.

Soon after Mom's lung cancer diagnosis, I traveled to Seattle more frequently to help with implementing decisions. It was such a new, painful reality. I wanted to be there whenever I could. My incredible manager adjusted my forty hour work week down to thirty-five hours. They gave me leave for the last five hour shift, and I used this time to fly to Seattle every weekend.

Mom put up a pretty good fight to protest me coming down each weekend. She was concerned about the disruption to my family life in Anchorage. I was working close to full time, and I would be leaving my husband and seven-year-old son on my days off. I explained I just wanted to make sure her radiation appointments went smoothly and to take her shopping for easy-to-fix meals for treatment days.

While we visited, I listened to her concerns about how some things were going to work. She wondered how to reconcile the various doctor, hospital, and treatment bills with Medicare and her several insurance policies, since supplemental policies did not coordinate with Medicare at this time. Mom was meticulous with her bookkeeping, and generally the billing processes were pretty straightforward. She just did not feel confident about keeping track of the medical bills.

She talked in general terms of her concerns about staying on top of her regular tasks and routines. I did not tell her I would be back every week, and that I would "take care of everything." I just went to her appointments and took her shopping—only the things I said I would do. And I listened. I wanted her to feel safe talking about her worries, without being afraid someone would swoop in and run her life.

When I was back in Alaska, I called her every day, gleaned a few more concerns, skipped the next week's trip then returned to discreetly address a few of those concerns. When I came back the following week, I explained I had an idea to show her about the billing system. After she went to bed, I set up the system, brought everything up to date, and took a look at her mail. The next day, she was relieved to see it was all set up, and the ledger was current. I told her it was in my wheelhouse—I enjoyed it and would like to take care of that for her when I visited. From then on, the conversations about doing things for her were simple. I came down every week until the end. By day, we shared memories and built new ones. At night, I took care of business.

What if you do not know what your loved one needs?

These general suggestions may be a good place to start:

- **Shopping**: Before your next shopping trip, check with your loved one or their caregiver if they want you to pick anything up for them. Alternatively, help them order groceries and deliveries online.

- **Transportation**: Ask if you can drive them to an event where you are both invited. Offer a ride to a one-time or recurring appointment.

- **Medication Tracking**: Offer to set up a schedule and system for taking medications. Some pharmacies assist with pre-packaging medications into packets for patients on stabilized medication routines.

- **Occasional Meal Prep**: Offer to bring over that extra lasagna from the double batch you are making. Or, just surprise them with it—they can freeze it for later. Offer cards to a local food delivery service. DoorDash™ or Grubhub™ are two food delivery apps you can use to deliver food to your loved one.

- **Pet Care**: Offer to walk their dog or care for their other pets.

- **Personal Hygiene**: Offer whatever the two of you are comfortable with, such as helping with washing and drying their hair.

- **Kids' Day Out**: If there are kids still at home, offer to bring them out of the house for a day. Take them on a bike ride, picnic, ball game, movie, or hike. This gives your loved one some time to themselves.

- **Caregiver Break Night**: Offer to take the night shift. Once a week, spend the night and be the person to take the night calls for assistance. This gives the caregiver an uninterrupted night of sleep—a huge help!

- **Volunteer Organizer**: Not all of us are domestic goddesses or comfortable with one-on-one caregiving. If your loved one is a member of an organization such as a church, work group, or Rotary Club that has expressed their desire to help, a volunteer can coordinate people to provide support. A good person for this role is someone who loves to organize. They can talk to your loved one or the caregiver about what type of help they might need on a daily, weekly, or as-needed basis. This person can coordinate their group to fulfill these needs and post a calendar to organize communication.

For example, "In November, Bill will stay over Wednesday nights. John has volunteered to shovel the driveway when snow accumulates. Pat and Carrie will alternate weekends to take the kids on Saturday mornings from eleven to three o'clock. George and Cal will come over this week to finish safety-proofing the house. Dave will be on call for minor house maintenance emergencies. Their neighbor Jennifer will walk the dog."

Organizing and communicating with everyone involved is crucial to minimizing stress. A perfect job for their Type A friend.

> **A Note of Caution**: Before taking up tasks to support your loved one, make sure they or their caregiver have accepted your offers to help. Give them the chance for input first. Otherwise, they may misconstrue your efforts as overbearing.

In addition to these general suggestions, consider how you can help your loved one or their caretaker with their specific needs. Take a moment to think about their routines, chores, and things they enjoy that they might need help doing.

These tasks could be small, like filling the empty bird feeder you know they enjoy watching. Recall conversations when they may have mentioned something that bothered them, and consider ways to help them with it. For example, if they mentioned missing getting their hair cut, ask their barber or hairdresser if they would make a house call. If they do not do house calls, ask them to recommend someone who does. You can also contact a local nursing home and see who visits them to provide hair care. Think outside the box.

If you are feeling stuck and cannot think of anything in their routine, consider your own routine for ideas. What tasks, chores, and daily routines take up your time and energy that you would appreciate help with? These may be ways to support your loved one.

As you think of these things, or if they come up in conversation with your loved one, jot them down here:

_____

_____

_____

_____

_____

_____

_____

_____

_____

To Wrap It Up: Being present in your loved one's life does not require any specific amount of time or effort. Acts of support are most effective when they come from a genuine place of love. Check in with yourself and do what you can. If they are comfortable connecting with you on an emotional level, inviting them to open up about their fears and challenges can help you support them. Regardless of your role, try to understand what a peaceful passing for your loved one means. Consider how you can help give them this experience.

With a few short words, my world changed. My mom's cancer diagnosis meant I had to navigate my own emotions as well as step up to help her in new ways. In the blink of an eye, my identity changed. My thoughts raced—how would I handle what comes next?

PART 3

AFTER THE WORDS YOU NEVER WANTED TO HEAR

Chapter 7
How to Get Past This Moment

In the first hours, days, and weeks of this new reality, what do you say? What can you do?

"Patty, in all my years as an oncologist, I never told a person they had cancer that didn't already know it in at least some very small part of their soul. And because this is their reality, they can acknowledge it in a different way than their loved ones." Somehow, this comment from Mom's doctor helped—to think she might be handling this news better than me.

He was right, again. Mom could see things for what they were. I did not want to see things as they were. It felt like that would mean I was okay with it. Nonetheless, I knew I needed to accept her requests as if this were a normal time just like any other—as if she were sending me to the store with a grocery list. But it took a lot of acting. I came to understand that these feelings are common for people who are facing a terminal diagnosis of their loved one.

Mom realized the time was fast approaching that she would not have control of her life as she knew it. She wanted to exercise her options and make decisions while she could. Following the doctor's advice, I fulfilled Mom's requests to select a casket and flowers, plan a wake, and call my siblings to her, so she could extract a pledge of support, peace, and love for each other for eternity. We were discovering what she would come to think of as a good death. I took on a new role: comforter. I did not want to be the one *she* needed to support.

On one of the worst days of their life, being with your loved one can be very comforting for them, and painful for you. There is no way to know the full range of emotions they are experiencing—including complete numbness. A protective fog can set in after learning their diagnosis. This is one reason doctors do not usually ask for decisions immediately. In fact, they may discourage making any major decisions until some time has passed. There are many decisions to make, but not on this first day.

The best way you can help is listening to your loved one and letting them lead. They may feel traumatized. You may see a variety of reactions. If there are quiet times, do not feel the need to fill them with conversation. Your loved one may feel disconnected from the reality they knew before, or they may find comfort being grounded by routine. They may want support nearby for the day, or they may want to be alone with a bowl of popcorn and a distracting movie. During the first days after the confirmation of a life-limiting illness, self-care is frequently the first casualty. Thoughts of nutrition, hydration, and good rest do not make it through the fog. Offering and making these things readily available without well-intentioned lectures will help. Try to make whatever they need happen.

As you try to understand what they need, learning how to speak respectfully with a person entering their final stage of life becomes an essential skill. How do you learn how to do this?

CHAPTER 8
CONVERSATIONS TO HAVE AND NOT HAVE

When your loved one is dying, their view of life can change significantly. Their outlook may be very different from yours or any other person in their life who is not facing their own mortality. It is important to not project your feelings onto your dying loved one. Loving them does not give you the ability to know what is best for them or how they feel. Wanting them to be okay is totally different from saying, "You'll get through this, it's going to be all right," or "A positive outlook always helps."[1]

Here are some other types of conversations that might only serve you and not comfort them:

- Your religious views

- How other people you know fared with a similar illness

- Your internet research on their illness, prognosis, or treatments

- What they should do, think, or feel

After the fog starts to lift, your loved one may be ready to ask questions. An important question for them to consider is "How much do I want to know?"

Some want to know every detail of their treatment options.

If your loved one wants to know as many details as possible, here are examples of questions they might want to ask their doctor:

- What will this form of treatment do?

- Will it help them live longer or feel better?

- What are the side effects?

- What might the disease progression look like?

- When should they know if the treatment is working?

- What else can they try if this treatment does not work?

- How uncomfortable will they be?

- How much help will they need?

Others may only want to know when they need to make decisions about treatments, and what the change in prognosis might be with treatment options.[2]

Still others may feel anxious and not want to be part of these discussions. They ask the doctor to keep their chosen person informed about treatment effectiveness, changes, and prognosis. Throughout the course of the illness, this decision may change—but it must be their decision.

As a Type A personality, while I was with my mom in the doctor's office, quietly listening to what I considered unhelpful information, my frustration meter was discreetly off the chart. Mom asked no questions, and the doctor did not ask if she had any. Only after he sent Mom to the front desk to make appointments, leaving the doctor and I alone in the office, was I able to bombard him with questions.

I am grateful something prevented me from blurting my questions out in front of Mom. The doctor acted respectfully, allowing her the time to decide what she was prepared to hear. Although I felt strongly that knowledge was essential to preparing for things to come, it was not my right to force Mom to take part in a discussion she did not want to have yet, if ever. She had decided that she wanted me to receive the information.

My takeaway—just listen to your loved one. Try to tune into what they are ready to face. Only they will know when they are ready to learn their options. Only they will know when they are prepared for the onslaught of well-wishes and condolences, or the barrage of questions and advice.

When your loved one is ready to tell others about their diagnosis, they will decide when, how, and who. They may call on you to help with this process, or not. It is not appropriate to share this news or any updates without their permission. If you are a co-worker of a terminally ill friend, discretion is important in the workplace. Gossip can be hurtful.

Once they have spoken personally with the people they want to tell first, they may want to use group emails or social media to update their friends and family. Some people use private family Facebook groups or pages. Joining a Facebook support group or creating a blog are other outlets. You or another volunteer may offer to set up or manage these communications.

> Visit the Resources section of this book to learn more about a website called CaringBridge, built to help people with medical conditions communicate with their loved ones.[3]

Where you are in the line of "who was told when" is insignificant. So do not let it become a personal issue. Your loved one may have an order in mind, but do not assume their reasons. Keep the big picture in mind and priorities clear. Focus on how to manage your feelings and support your loved one. Be careful not to place them in the role of consoling you.

> **To Wrap It Up**: Everyone is unique in how they respond to the challenges of terminal illness or old age frailty. Do not make assumptions. Do not be the person they need to support while they face the reality of their life ending. Instead, ask what they need—food, company, quiet. Be mindful of the needs of other household members as well.

Your loved one's stage of life and stage of illness can influence how to help them through a peaceful end-of-life experience. Connection and compassion are profound at any stage. You just want to meet them where they are. So, in what stage is your loved one?

PART 4

PERSPECTIVES FROM DIFFERENT STAGES OF LIFE

Seek first to understand, then to be understood.

—Dr. Steven R. Covey

CHAPTER 9
STORIES BEHIND DECISIONS

E ach person's life story is unique. When a person enters their final stage of life, their values, perspectives, and experiences influence the decisions they make. Throughout this book, you will read stories of people at different stages of life who faced their deaths in ways that fit them best. To support your loved one, you can learn how their personal life path impacts the decisions they make at this chapter.

Fifteen years earlier, my father-in-law Jack suffered kidney failure and began the arduous regimen of dialysis. On the transplant list for what seemed like years, his health was failing, as he approached the age limit for transplants. Short of the miracle of an immediate donor match, Jack would not be receiving a transplant. His sixty-two-year-old brother-in-law was tested and matched for the transplant. Everything was perfect—for a minute.

During final screenings and prep for the transplant, Jack had a cardiac incident that culminated in a seven-way bypass. The lengthy surgery was a success, but first assessments in the recovery room indicated a global stroke had occurred during surgery. Reluctantly, the doctors agreed to delay the transplant and reevaluate his transplant viability after rehabilitation therapy. A strong-willed, almost obstinate man, Jack worked hard and satisfied the surgeon's requirements to receive his transplant later that spring.

He overcame many obstacles during his lifetime, including skin cancer. Now, as an organ transplant patient, he lived with new challenges. Yet Jack was not going to let this keep him from a full and rewarding final chapter. Jack kept his zest for life through it all. When his transplanted kidney began to fail, he was admitted for evaluation, where they discovered blood cancer and end-stage renal disease.

Jack's many friends and family loved him dearly. He cherished his time and life with them. The man I knew would not walk away from them if he had a choice. With the family waiting just outside his open hospital door, we could hear the doctor explain the prognosis and options to my father and mother-in-law. Now, a seemingly slightly smaller, frail man lying in that bed listened without question or comment. An unfamiliar expression and then a slight smile—one I had never seen before—came over his face. He had just been told his kidney had stopped functioning, and they needed to start dialysis that day. The blood cancer would require transfusions twice a week. His response was "I'm not ready to go back on dialysis, I want to go home and think about it for a few days." But he didn't have a few days.

Seeing that unfamiliar expression and very thin smile, I thought Jack was not registering what they said. I thought he meant that he felt overwhelmed and needed time to process it all. In reality, my father-in-law understood perfectly. He was tired. He felt he had had a good life. He did not want to spend the short time he had left in treatments. He had made his decision.

Your loved one's stage of life can influence many of their decisions. A younger person may consider more rounds of treatment or join drug trials to extend their time. It can be a quantity-versus-quality decision, perhaps allowing them to have a little more time with their young children or to attend a milestone event such as a wedding or graduation. A person who has led a long and full life may decide against painful or debilitating treatments in order to spend a peaceful time with friends and family who shared a lifetime of experiences with them. They may opt not to fill their time with treatments, appointments, and diminishing quality of life.

At any stage of life, these decisions can be difficult. With the internal noise of so many things to consider, sometimes an attempt to be supportive can inadvertently achieve the opposite. In your conversations or body language, they might hear labels, judgements, or attempts to influence their choices. Well-intentioned phrases can actually hurt to hear: "Don't give up," "You're so brave," "You're a fighter," "You're a hero," "Don't quit," or "You're going to be okay." For instance, if they change their treatment decision, are they not brave? A hero? A fighter? They know they are dying. However they choose their personal path for their remaining days, it is important to respect their autonomy. Meet them where they are.

For my friend Lianne, diagnosed with an aggressive cancer, it was an easy choice. She had always been healthy and energetic. Lianne had already overcome serious odds when she survived a car accident that took her husband's life and put her in intensive care for eight days. She was a fighter.

Her son Doug would be starting his first year at college in a few weeks. This was a happy and exciting time in his life. They were best friends, staying up for many a late night discussing choices, hopes, dreams, and possible futures. Lianne did not want to miss sending her son off to college—and more importantly, she did not want to leave her only child without any parents.

Though he was not encouraging, her oncologist gave her options to consider. To Lianne, aggressive cancer meant aggressive treatment. They started treatments, and she started researching. The side effects of the treatments were somewhere between uncomfortable and debilitating. She felt discouraged finding a lot of information, but not finding anything her doctor had not already explained to her.

Lianne was not able to attend any of the events Doug participated in during the first quarter of his freshman year, but they spent a nice Christmas break together. Doug was surprised to see how tired and frail his mom seemed, but they did not have any serious discussions about it. She saved those for close friends. She had a break in treatments over the holidays. Then, she would be reevaluated and discuss next steps with her doctor. Lianne did not rally as much as she had hoped she would, and the treatments were not effective. The next appointment left the discussion of new or experimental treatments behind and moved into realistic expectations.

Lianne told me the discussion was not a shock. It seemed like a natural progression that she had already begun in her mindset. She said, "There was a weird kind of relief, like we were both agreeing it was time to change our focus and to start the next part of life." She and her doctor had a good discussion about new goals and how to get as close as possible to them.

When Doug came home at spring break, he and Lianne had a long, difficult, and loving conversation with Lianne's parents. Her new goal was to be present in Doug's life as long as she could, with as much quality of life as they could create together. This young man was wise beyond his years, though sometimes, you might see the little boy with tears on his cheeks out of his mom's view. Respecting her wishes—and acknowledging she was still in charge—he reluctantly returned to school for the remainder of the last quarter. Still holding steadfast to her super organized Type A personality, Lianne enlisted support to complete her mission. While Doug was finishing the school year, she was preparing to leave a part of herself that would go with Doug throughout his life.

She wanted to share what she thought she had a full lifetime to share. She wanted to teach her son about the woman who brought him into the world and loved him fiercely even before his first breath. Lianne was creating a **loving will**, a compilation of personal stories, thoughts, feelings, history, memories, and prized possessions meant for one person.[1] A loving will shares what can only come from one person's soul to another. With her limited energy, she enlisted her army of three friends to work on preparations for the transition, as she called it, while she completed her loving will and wrote her **legacy letter**, also known as an **ethical will**. Lianne addressed her legacy letter to all her heirs, friends, and family, and it shared her values, life lessons, regrets, and gratitude.

Other friends came by, and as grateful as Lianne was, certain visits seemed to drain her physically or emotionally. Always gracious and appreciative, she shared with me that conversations where she found herself fielding many questions left her feeling like she was justifying her decisions. Some visitors offered unsolicited advice, like Lianne should insist Doug come home to spend as much time as possible with her. There were insensitive questions about what kind of cancer she had, where it was in her body, and what timeline did the doctor discuss. There was superficial flattery about how good she looked. We sort of chuckled at that. Because we accepted this reality and spoke candidly about what she was experiencing, we shared a gallows sense of humor. A beautiful woman inside and out, but "without a good hair day in months," as she said, with thin pale skin and thirty pounds lighter than her usual fit figure, we both laughingly acknowledged—she'd looked better. Their comments were not supportive, they were invasive, insincere, and sometimes hurtful.

Lianne knew there was no intent to hurt her. Her friends thought they were being supportive and showing an interest. So she refocused and continued her preparations, determined to complete her loving will for Doug before he returned from college. Sometimes Lianne would want to talk about the recollections she was recording, or to have one of us help find certain treasures to set aside. But she wanted to do as much of this herself as she could.

When Doug came home from college in June, Lianne presented a neatly wrapped box that contained her loving will, a few of her smaller treasures—her wedding rings, her great-grandfather's gavel from the first trial he adjudicated, and others. She gave Doug pictures of art and other items in her house that listed their locations in the home and explained their special meaning and history. For a few hours every day, they would read parts of the loving will. Doug would ask questions, and Lianne would expand on some of her stories. When they came to her music section, they played the songs she listed and talked about their special meaning to Lianne. Her "army" had been able to locate and download these songs—just in case he was curious—and he was. It included the song that she and his dad dubbed "their song," the music played at their wedding, the music played at his dad's funeral service, and the lullabies she sang to him as a baby. We recorded her singing those lullabies to him again and put it on a thumb drive with the rest of the songs.

Doug and Lianne had been revisiting some of the stories in her living room when I stopped by for a quick visit. At first I thought, *Uh oh, this is going to be a sad visit.* I was wrong. It started with Doug—with a huge and incredulous grin—asking me all about if I knew his mom went here and there, and that she did this and that . . . and the storytelling commenced. Not only did we laugh, cry, and amaze each other—we sparked more revelations and recollections with Lianne's other friends over the next few months. Why hadn't we done this before?

July was the beginning of the hard times. Lianne wanted to complete one more project while she still had the ability. She recorded a letter to Doug and had it transcribed. When she asked me to give it to Doug after her service, she shared some of what she included in it. In this letter, she told him how proud she had always been of him. She told him about the times he revealed his values and strengths, and how she knew he would overcome the trials and tribulations that come to everyone. It was full of love and inspiration.

As they enter their dying process, your loved one will face decisions that are deeply personal. It is a gift to listen to them and support their decisions about what is best for them at this stage. Another part of this process involves supporting them as they determine how they want to leave their legacy. This can be a beautiful experience that brings you close together in ways that preserve your loving bond forever. How do you create a legacy that honors them best?

CHAPTER 10
ECHOES OF A LIFE WELL LIVED

At the end of life, many people consider what they would like to leave behind—lessons they have learned, fun family stories, personal messages to family members and friends, favorite recipes, music, and more. Brainstorm ideas with your loved one to see what matters most to them.

> Supporting your loved one's quest for a good end-of-life experience includes acknowledging and honoring their life.

You can help your loved one complete several projects to reassure them that their wisdom, story, and messages will survive beyond their physical life. Timing is everything in these projects. They may not be ready for these reflections, or they may want to start, and then put it aside for a bit. They may never choose to do any of these projects. It is their decision what they want to do with their time. If they ask for help completing any of these projects, working on them together can be among the most profound gifts you can give them and their family.

Here are some projects you can offer to help with:

- **Ethical Will or Legacy Letter**: You can offer to help your loved one write a personal letter to their family or heirs. It is an opportunity to pass on their values, express their powerful life lessons, regrets, gratitude, and more.[2] Dr. Barry Baines, author of *Ethical Wills:*

Putting Your Values on Paper, has also created a writing guide and workbook that can assist you in organizing and writing an ethical will.

Visit everplans.com for a worksheet to compose an ethical will.

- **Private Letter**: Help your loved one write a letter to someone with whom they want to share their last thoughts. They may write several letters or notes that you could transcribe and mail or deliver for them.

- **Loving Will**: Help your loved one put together their loving will, a collection of stories, thoughts, feelings, wishes, dreams, history, prized possessions, favorite memories, and blessings that they want to pass on to each of their loved ones individually. If your loved one is still active and would like to do this, consider starting your own loving will. This can be a rewarding project that you both can set aside time to work on together. You can begin your loving will and amend it throughout your life. This project can be an emotional experience. Take time to think about each item or person and capture the good you see in them. Hearing what you thought was good in them might help them see a side of themselves they may have never acknowledged before. The Loving Will Project was created by Bonnie Nichols, Director of Organizational Experience and her Spiritual Care Team at Central Peninsula General Hospital, in Soldotna, Alaska. Components of this project have been reprinted with permission by Ms. Nichols.

My grandmother gave her grandchildren a loving will when our grandfather passed away. They were married for over sixty years. She wrote the story of how they met, their hardships, and blessings throughout their lives together. It included pictures of him as a marine in World War I, another in uniform as a conductor for the Great Northern Railroad, and finally a picture of them at their fiftieth wedding anniversary. We also received gold-etched crystal gifts they were given on their golden anniversary. Grandma enjoyed the experience of writing about the most important era of her life—and her joy at sharing all of this became another gift itself.

Grandma and her two sisters came together to create a notebook telling the stories of their family's early history, including the trials of coming out West by wagon train in the late 1800s, where they encountered plagues, floods, famine, and robbers. They told the story of their little brother that was born and died on the journey. The stories were full of life lessons, hardship, and gratitude. Their grandchildren appreciated the gift of this legacy notebook. Their histories and experiences had never been shared before, for no particular reason. All conversations seemed to be about the here and now. Without these recollections, a treasure would be lost. Grandma died not long after they finished the notebook.

Creating a loving will or legacy letter can be as rewarding to the writer as the reader. Here are the basics, for your loved one to get started.

To start creating a loving will, label an envelope or computer folder. This is your loved one's collection spot where they can place or list special messages, objects, and treasures. Suggest your loved one keep in mind one thing they want each person to know.

Help them list all the people who played a significant role in their life. You can include people who were especially kind and even those who were unkind.

Ask your loved one how they want to share their loving will with each special person in their life. With technology today, they have a choice to write, record video, or record audio of their personal sentiments, messages, observations, and hopes for their family and friends. If their loving will mentions objects, pictures, or recipes, be sure to record their locations and which people your loved one would like to receive them.

A loving will is not a legal document, but some people give it to their attorney or executor to distribute like their last will and testament. But your loved one does not have to wait until death to provide these gifts of loving legacy. They can choose any time they feel is appropriate. Here are some ideas for your loved one to consider as they begin their loving will.

Reflections on the Special People in Their Life

Choose one person and try out these prompts. Your loved one may write their thoughts in this table, or you may ask them these questions and write for them:

What is one word that describes them best? Try one-word descriptors like kind, generous, protector, clown, etc.	
What are your favorite memories with them?	
What has their presence meant in your life?	
How would you describe them in your own unique way?	
What are all the qualities you love and admire in them?	

Precious Objects

Passing mementos down to loved ones can be very powerful for both giver and receiver. Include a short story or memory about how each of these objects came into their possession. The unique meaning they hold can make these special treasures even more meaningful to the person receiving them.

Here are some ideas to ask your loved one:

Do you have a story about a piece of jewelry that was created just for you?	
Do you have handmade items, like a grandmother's quilt, that you want to hand down?	
Do the decorations in your home, such as artwork on the walls, hold special meaning?	

You can tape a note on the back of each item or add notes to each item on their list. This list can be long, so start with the item they think is most precious and write its story first.

Legendary Stories

It is a heartening experience to sit around a dinner table with family members after a loved one passes and listen to incredibly funny stories and happy memories of that person. These are the stories you can pass on to future generations. Your loved one's stories will likely take much more space than provided. Use the adjacent box to make notes of which stories they want to include. Later, you can help them write or record them.

Try asking your loved one these prompts:

What stories show how you or your ancestry persevered through challenging times—struggles, achievements, and lessons learned?	
What are some funny stories from your life?	
What stories do you want to be sure are remembered?	
What stories do you want to pass on to loved ones?	

Favorite Books, Authors, and Music

These works of art can leave a trail for family to follow and enjoy their connection to your loved one.

Try the following questions:

Was there an author or artist who shaped your outlook in life?	
Was there a particular poem or poet who gave you hope during a particularly challenging time?	
Do you have a favorite scripture or sacred text?	
Was there a favorite musician, album, or song you listened to when you fell in love?	
Did you keep a journal that you want to share with family that might help them as they move through life?	

Photos

After a loved one passes, pictures of them become their family's most beloved treasures.

Here are some steps you can take to preserve family photos:

- Collect loose family photos and label them with names, dates, and places.

- Collect photos into groups and label their categories.

- Take lots of pictures on your next trip or family gathering and have them made into a photobook, or use the photos already on your computer. This might be a great place to enlist the help of a young family member.

> Visit snapfish.com, shutterfly.com, or mixbook.com for tools to upload images straight from your computer and make photobooks.

Favorite Recipes

Family traditions are closely tied to memories of specially prepared foods. This is an opportunity to pass on favorite recipes that have fond memories associated with them.

Ask your loved one the following:

Is there a family cookbook?	
Do you have a card file or computer file with recipes earmarked for special occasions, friends, and/or family? If so, where is this located?	

My friend Kellene combined photos and recipes into one photobook. After Kellene's mom passed, she wanted to make sure her siblings had copies of their mother's recipes. Many of these were family favorites and part of long standing traditions. Some were made especially for a family member who declared that particular dish as their favorite. Kellene collected recipes and pictures of family gatherings that showed them enjoying these dishes. In the photobook, she placed each recipe next to a picture of their family enjoying that dish. When she could not find a photo showing them enjoying a certain dish, she would use a picture of her mom with the person she made the dish for, or a photo of her cooking. She created lifetime treasures to pass on the beloved recipes and memories.

Regrets and Unfinished Business

Misunderstandings in families and friendships can happen in many ways. A wrong word, a heated debate, or not having all the information can lead to a communication breakdown. Here is the opportunity to rebuild those bridges. Communicate what you have wanted to share, but did not know how—until now. This can invite your loved one to do the same with you and other people in their life.

> **To Wrap It Up**: It is easy to assume our loved ones see the same world, hear the same messages, and have the same feelings as we do. Yet that cannot ever be completely true. Each of our lives and deaths is unique. No matter how much we love a person or share their lives, we are still only observers. Helping your loved one record their legacy can be a precious time when you listen and learn more about them than ever before. You can create rich memories together to carry with you throughout your lifetime.

No matter what stage of life your loved one is in, they have many decisions to make. Some will be critical, some inconsequential. This is not a time to attempt to influence or judge. So what is it time for?

PART 5

DECISIONS TO MAKE, COMMUNICATE, AND RECORD

CHAPTER 11

ADVANCE DIRECTIVES, WILLS, AND TRUSTS

We would all like to believe we will have a long, healthy, active life until the day we die—but what if we don't?

No matter what your role is, how old you are, or what your health status is, this chapter is for you.

If you are over the age of eighteen, it is important to complete your **advance directive**, sometimes called a **living will**. In some states, an advance directive and a living will are considered the same thing. An advance directive is a legal document that provides guidance to your loved ones and health care team by stating your medical care preferences in advance of any event in which you lose the capacity to make decisions for yourself. The advance directive has two main components: the **living will** and the designation of a **medical power of attorney**, sometimes known as a health care power of attorney.[1] Frequently people include their organ donation preference and other stipulations. Visit the Resources section of this book for more information.

In an ideal world, you could make these decisions leisurely, in casual conversation with friends and family. But if an accident or sudden illness occurs, and you have not made your wishes known in a living will, your medical decisions could be made by someone you would not have chosen to make them. Or, the family member who steps in to make decisions on your behalf may anguish over whether they made the decision you would want. This can leave you and your family in a vulnerable position and add to the stress.

If you are the primary caregiver, you need to know what choices are available and what decisions must be made. If you are a close family member or someone your loved one has chosen to help carry out their wishes, it will be helpful to know the types of decisions they may be facing. Making these decisions and preparations now clears the path for yourself and your loved ones in the future.

Tomorrow is promised to no one.

—Proverbs 27:1

Many people have had their ability to determine how they want to live—and how they want to die—taken away long before they imagined.

Everett, a young man who came into our family as a teenager in the foster care system, was already too familiar with pain—both physical and emotional. It was hard on him to be away from his community, and among other challenges, he suffered from rheumatoid arthritis that required regular medication for the pain. As the newest member of the family, Everett did well in his new environment. Knowing he was supported and loved, he thrived. Like the rest of the young adults in the family, he was taught skills to help him be independent and manage his life. The goal was to send the young adults into the world with all the knowledge and insights we could share, to help them make good decisions and keep them safe. Yet discussions about advance directives were not part of these conversations. Excitement and anticipation dominated the atmosphere whenever one of the young people grew old enough to step into the world on their own. No one thought about the worst-case scenarios that an advance directive would have prepared us to navigate. Had we thought about what a significant impact this could make in our lives—in Everett's life—we would have encouraged him to designate a medical power of attorney when he turned eighteen. Instead, the unthinkable happened.

One evening, Everett was riding his bike when he was struck by a car and left with life-threatening injuries. He was eighteen years old. EMTs transported the critically injured young man to the hospital, where he was intubated while in a coma. Though Everett was eighteen, he was still considered under state care. Even as his foster family, we had no authority to advocate for what we believed would have been his wishes. An advance directive was required. His status remained unchanged for several weeks, and the doctors indicated they did not expect any significant change in his condition. It was the state's decision to send him to a long-term care facility in a city accessible only by plane, two hours away, where nobody knew him. Three years later, Everett is still there, in the same condition.

It is paradoxical that your loved one has so many decisions to make at the very time it may feel they have the least control. Some may have considered these decisions before, and others may be completely caught off guard. In either case, the last thing they need is a firehose full of questions  drowning them. If you are part of their inner circle trying to help with this daunting task, the first step is establishing your priorities: to help provide peace of mind and support their autonomy while helping them go through this process. It is important to resist the temptation of seeing this as a long list of chores to get done.

Hopefully, the directives on these forms come from a series of conversations you can have over time. As their health or other circumstances change, they may alter some of these choices. As long as your loved one is able to make their own decisions, they can change any portion of these, or toss the whole thing.

To ensure your loved one's final wishes are respected, they need to communicate key decisions. They will need to choose, and identify in the advance directive, a trusted individual who will use specific legal documents to help make this happen. These documents are free, available online, and some are state-specific. Some require a notary. None require an attorney, but an attorney can be helpful.

The advance directive is one of the state-specific documents. It is available online from several sources, and you can download it specifying your state. You can also obtain it from your attorney, doctor, or hospital.

A living will is probably the most important communication tool available. It allows you to communicate the level of care you want. This form details your wishes *if you are no longer able to communicate them*. It spells out what approach to treatment you want, whether an aggressive curative approach or comfort care, which provides comfort for the dying process, foregoing attempts at recovery. It may specify which interventions you want, such as palliative care, medications, artificial nutrition, hydration, resuscitation, dialysis, ventilation, and more.

When a person can no longer communicate their wishes, their family may not know what they would want. Before your loved one decides which measures they want, it is helpful for them to discuss the ramifications of these decisions with their doctor.

How Do You Start the Conversation?

Central Peninsula General Hospital's care team in Soldotna, Alaska, has created "Conversation Cues."[2] This set of questions helps start discussions about what matters to your loved one. It is written in the format of a survey, where next to each topic, they can rate its level of importance to them. As I read through this, it was easy to see the value in learning these wishes as early as possible. The Conversation Cues give you information to provide for your loved one's physical wishes and to nurture their sense of self, their emotional and spiritual sides, and their autonomy. Here is a copy of the Conversation Cues.

Visit the Resources section for the link to download your own inventory. This is not part of an advance directive, but helps identify what is important to your loved one.

Conversation Cues

If you need to make healthcare decisions on my behalf, this is what matters to me:	Very Important	Somewhat Important	Not Important
Human touch and voice, even if I can't or don't appear to respond.			
Be able to say goodbye to family and loved ones.			
Have my values, beliefs, and cultural priorities known and respected.			
Know who I am, where I am, and who I am with.			
Live as long as possible.			
Not be short of breath.			
Be free from anxiety.			
Be free from pain.			
To not hallucinate.			
Be physically comfortable (moist lips and mouth, a cold compress if I have a fever, keep me clean, change sheets and clothing regularly and when needed, etc.)			
To be treated with respect and dignity.			
Have family and friends know and respect my wishes, even if they are not decisions they would make.			

If you need to make healthcare decisions on my behalf, this is what matters to me:	Very Important	Somewhat Important	Not Important
To feel that my life has had meaning and purpose.			
Have my family prepared for my death.			
Have my financial affairs in order.			
Some quiet time alone.			
Time with my spiritual advisor or chaplain.			
Be able to talk with my doctor honestly about my health and options.			
Have my funeral arrangements made.			
Not being a burden to my family.			
To die at home.			
To be able to support others.			
If I am placed on Comfort Care, I would like a companion, so I will not be alone if friends or family cannot be with me.			

An article from the Journal of the American Medical Association, a report from the Institute of Medicine, and a review from a University of California San Diego School of Medicine research team found the consensus that there is no one definition of a "good death," but there are between nine and twelve key principles that characterize one. The above inventory presents many of these principles.

Nurses support the wishes listed in the Conversation Cues chart. The *American Journal of Nursing* published "The Dying Patient's Bill of Rights" which establishes that a dying person has the following rights:[3]

- To be treated as a living human being until death

- To maintain a sense of hopefulness, however changing its focus may be

- To be cared for by those who can maintain a sense of hopefulness, however changing this might be

- To express feelings and emotions about approaching death in their own way

- To participate in decisions concerning their care

- To expect continuing medical and nursing attention even though "cure" goals have been changed to "comfort" goals

- Not to die alone

- To be free from pain

- To have their questions answered honestly

- Not to be deceived

- To have help accepting death

- To die in peace and dignity

- To retain individuality and not be judged for decisions that may be contrary to the beliefs of others

- To discuss and enlarge religious and/or spiritual experiences

- To expect that the sanctity of the human body will be respected after death

- To be cared for by caring, sensitive, knowledgeable people who will attempt to understand their needs

If you are their health care agent, you must advocate for your loved one and emphasize issues of importance with their health care team, both personal and professional. Some hospitals and other health care facilities do not have palliative care or hospice training. If you witness your loved one's wishes, rights, and advance directives not being followed, you must be your loved one's voice.

Your loved one may state their preferences for the following in their advance directive:

- **Health Care Agent** or **Medical Power of Attorney**: Most states have limitations on who may be elected for this role, such as disallowing their doctor or anyone who works for their health care system. This person is responsible for enforcing the wishes in their advance directive. If your loved one does not complete an advance directive, their medical power of attorney and their health care provider should discuss the rights and responsibilities of this position and decisions they may be called on to make. Some states require a separate form to designate someone for this position.

- **Organ Donation**: Another preference they can state in an advance directive is whether or not they want to be an organ door, though this is not required in an advance directive. They may choose to donate any or all of their organs to people in need, or they may choose to donate their body to medical science. If they choose to die at home, vital organs like the heart, lungs, kidneys, and liver are not viable for transplant because they must be harvested immediately. In order to donate these organs for transplant to help living people, they would need to die in a facility where medical intervention is possible. However, certain organs can still be donated for scientific research and educational purposes, if your loved one opts to die at home. Corneas can be donated several hours after death. Tissues such as skin, bones, tendons, and heart valves can be donated within twenty-four hours after death. Whole body donations typically must be pre-arranged. For a whole body donation, the deceased remains are received by the **Anatomy Bequest Program** either at the time of death or immediately after the funeral. Their health care team, medical power of attorney, and family should be aware of their desire to be a donor, and the donor should always have their donor card on them.

It is important for family and loved ones to know that when an organ donor dies in the hospital, they will be taken away immediately. It may ease the sorrow of not having more time to say goodbye to know organ donors can save up to eight lives and enhance the lives of seventy-five more people.

The advance directive must be signed by two witnesses. Neither can be the health care agent, and/or be notarized, depending on specific state requirements. Several organizations offer assistance in preparing your advance directive either on paper or digitally. They can also store it in the cloud, along with any other health care directives that you complete. These services are secure, and you can access them from any location with internet connection. Your loved one can easily update or remove them.

A growing number of organizations provide these services:

- **Five Wishes**: Five Wishes is a holistic approach to advance care planning. The forms prompt us to complete the advance directive to communicate our specific wishes for our physical, emotional, and spiritual care. Five Wishes offers planning guidance in booklet or digital form. There is a small fee.

- **My Directives:** you can then store your documents with My Directives, where they will be accessible to your family or health care providers, as you direct. My Directives also offers the necessary forms for the advance directive, focusing on the legal aspects. If you choose to use forms from other sources, you can upload your forms and use My Directives' cloud storage for free.

- **U.S. Advance Care Plan Registry**: You can also store your forms on USACPR for a fee.

There are links to these organizations websites in the resource section.

Before making decisions about life-sustaining treatment, it is helpful for your loved one to talk with their doctor about the expectations of their end-of-life care and what decisions they will have to make. It is important they understand the consequences of these decisions.

Here are some questions to keep in mind:

- What would their quality of life be like with or without a certain treatment?

- How would a certain treatment affect their life expectancy?

- If they begin a certain treatment, would this treatment continue for the duration of their lifetime, or would it be a temporary phase of treatment?

These can be difficult conversations, but they are worthwhile. They can assure your loved one receives the end-of-life care they want.

Whether in a health care facility or at home, medical responders are required to follow mandated protocol. Yet this protocol may be the opposite of your loved one's wishes. To make sure their wishes about life-sustaining treatment are met, your loved one must make records of their decisions easily accessible to their advocates and health care team, in case they cannot communicate their wishes during a medical event.

Physicians Orders for Life *Sustaining* Treatment (POLST)

This form echoes the decisions made in an advance directive. Each state has its own form, so the name of this form may vary slightly. An advance directive is not necessary to have a POLST, but it is strongly recommended. Unlike an advance directive, which can be completed at any time and describes the type of care a person wants in the last days of their life, the POLST form is for people who are in critical distress and must make life-sustaining decisions. The options on the form ask specific measures they want or do not want. These range from taking any and all actions available to comfort care only. Filling out this form does not prevent care for other needs. For example, if EMTs are called to a home where someone has a POLST that states they do not want to be intubated, but they are having difficulty breathing, the EMTs can give them oxygen to make them comfortable until they get their breathing under control. It can be difficult to imagine situations that would require these decisions. Remember, most of these decisions kick in when your loved one cannot communicate. Preparing these forms is the key to making decisions that accurately reflect their wishes.

Their doctor will need to complete part of the POLST and sign it, in order for it to be valid. This requires a conversation with their doctor. It is a legal medical order that protects your loved one and their health care providers, and it carries more weight with first responders and other health care providers. There are several copies of this form. One copy will go home with your loved one. Keep it easily visible. You can tape this form somewhere obvious, like the refrigerator. It is a good idea to keep an additional copy with your loved one if they are traveling.

Because they share so many similarities, it might be difficult to see the differences between the advance directives and POLST forms. Yet it is helpful to complete both.

Key Differences between Advance Directive and POLST Forms:

	Advance Directive	POLST Form
Type of Document	Legal document	Medical order
Who should have the form?	Everybody over eighteen years old	Anyone at risk for a life-threatening clinical event because they have a serious life-limiting medical condition, including advanced frailty
Who completes the form?	Individual patient	Health care professional. Who can sign varies by state: https://polst.org/state-signature-requirements-pdf)
Does the form appoint a health care agent?	Yes	No
What does the form communicate?	General wishes about treatment	Specific medical orders
Are emergency personnel required to follow the form?	No	Yes

	Advance Directive	POLST Form
How easy is it to locate the form?	May be more difficult, depending on the patient's choices of where they keep their form, whether they have told anyone where it is, and whether they have given a copy to their health care surrogate or a health care professional to put into their chart or registry	Designed to be easy, with patient keeping the original single form, a copy in their medical record, and an additional copy in a registry
How often does the patient review the form?	Patient determines how often it is reviewed and/or updated	The doctor or physician assistant is responsible for reviewing the POLST with the patient or their surrogate when the following occurs: • The patient transfers to a different facility • A substantial change in their medical condition • The patient's goals of care or treatment preferences change

Make sure your loved one's primary doctor has copies of their advance directives. In addition, give copies of these two documents to their other doctors, durable power of attorney for medical care, and close family members.

Do Not Resuscitate (DNR)

When discussing end-of-life care, their doctor may ask if their heart stops, and they can only breathe by artificial means, do they want life-*saving* measures taken. If they do not want any attempt to resuscitate them, their doctor will issue a Do Not Resuscitate order (DNR), also known as Do Not Attempt to Resuscitate (DNAR), Allow Natural Death (AND), or No Code. This form is available from their doctor, hospital, clinic, or online. **The DNR requires a doctor's signature to be valid in most states.** Check with your health care provider or online, specifically for your state. Making this decision is difficult, but open and honest discussions with their doctor can provide a sense of autonomy and peace. These conversations might bring your loved one to the conclusion they do not want a DNR. They may decide they want every life-saving measure taken, as many times as possible. This is the default level of treatment.

It is worth mentioning, Cardio-Pulminary Resuscitation (CPR) is not what you see on television.

Though these details are not widely discussed, you can make better decisions with more information:

- In reality, CPR involves forceful chest compressions at least two inches deep at a rate of one hundred compressions per minute—much more vigorous than what is shown on TV.

- Only one or two out of ten cardiac victims survive.

- Survivors may experience permanent or temporary brain injuries that may manifest as speech difficulties, cognitive impairments, memory loss, weakness, and movement disorders.

- Immediate effects could result in physical trauma including internal bleeding, broken ribs, lung bruising, and airway damage.

- Minor discomforts such as nausea, dry mouth, headache, or sore throat recede within hours.

Additional forms of resuscitation include shocking the heart, medications, and inserting breathing tubes to keep a person alive.

Financial Durable Power of Attorney

This person is able to sign checks, make payments, complete other financial transactions, and generally manage financial affairs if your loved one is incapacitated. Some states have requirements for the protection of your loved one such as a letter from their doctor stating they are incapacitated or unable to take care of these responsibilities themselves. These powers are only in force while your loved one is alive and unable to direct someone in how they want their affairs executed. In selecting someone for this role, they should consider a person who has good money management skills and will look after your loved ones interests. This could be the same person selected as executor of their will.

Last Will and Testament

This legal document addresses guardianship and specifies how to disperse an individual's assets. To make this happen, your loved one must select a person who accepts the responsibilities of dispersing their assets and closing all business, legal, financial, and personal aspects of their life. This can be a monumental task even for modest estates. It is important to note, the will must authorize this person to manage online accounts, or they will not have access to them. Wills are not absolutely necessary, but they help specify the property your loved one wants to leave to people and entities such as charitable organizations. Wills are legal documents, but they can be contested. This is when attorneys enter the picture.

You can download a will or purchase a kit that your loved one can complete themselves and have notarized. This type of will may not allow for much customization and would work best for simple estates. Another option is consulting with an attorney. Many attorneys allot time to do pro bono work. Some offer thirty minute consultations for a nominal fee. If your loved one has a more complicated estate or is interested in a trust, retaining legal counsel is highly recommended.

For safekeeping, consider registering their will with a service such as the U.S Will Registry. This free and secure service confirms the existence and location of the will to anyone named in the permissions for their registry.

The following story shows the importance of making sure a will is registered, with extra copies for safekeeping.

John was family in every sense of the word but blood. An immigrant from Greece, John and Mom met when she moved from Washington to Anchorage, Alaska, in 1953, where she did not know anyone and did not have a job. Mom was quite adventurous. John and his wife Goldie were fairly well-to-do. They owned a few restaurants—he was a chef by trade—and they knew a lot of people in Anchorage. John gave Mom a job in one of his restaurants and took her under his wing. Mom met and married Dad, and they all lived through years of shared tragedies and triumphs, celebrations, and consolations. When Goldie died, John became an integral part of our family. All his living relatives were in Greece. John and Goldie never had kids, so my brother Andy and I became even more important to him.

In 1964, as Mom, Dad, and John were discussing plans for our move from Alaska to California, they decided John would move to California with us and handle the new restaurant they planned to start there. John sold his Anchorage restaurants, decided to keep his lake property in Alaska, and prepared to partially retire with us in California. We flew to Seattle, where we planned to meet Dad, and then we would continue on to California. When Dad died, everything stopped. We decided to stay in Seattle, where Mom's family lived. John stayed in Seattle with us part time and lived in Alaska part time. He doted on us. With his eternal love of cooking, he declared himself our in-house chef. He was our treasured friend and family member.

We never knew the extent of John's assets, but he offered to pay for expenses like my wedding or gifts of similar value for my brother Andy. He was extremely generous, despite our loving refusals to accept such large gifts. Evenso, John had a will in place for decades that named Andy and me as his sole heirs. He explained how we were to receive any and all properties, possessions, assets, and proceeds from them.

Mom and John would occasionally have spirited discussions. During one of these discussions, to make a point, Mom brought out her copy of John's will and tore it into tiny pieces. Of course, all was forgiven and forgotten the next day. Replacing Mom's copy of John's will was never a real concern. We all figured the next time John ran across his copy, we would have another copy made. Then, John had a heart attack and died. A few weeks after the service, Mom was trying to sort out what needed to be done to close John's estate. She could not find a copy of his will in his papers. We started down the rabbit hole. We tried to contact the attorney with whom John wrote his will, but the attorney had died the year before, and we were unable to locate the attorney's records. We went to John's bank to see if his will was in a safe deposit box, but without executor privileges, they could not tell us if he even had an account there—even though we knew he did. We checked with the court and discovered John's will was not registered. Eventually I contacted an attorney, only to be told there is nothing we could do. This is where the story ends. I know better now.

Revocable Trust

A revocable trust is a legal document that allows your loved one to manage their assets while they are alive and transfer their estate to their beneficiaries upon their death. This trust can be changed at any time but becomes irrevocable upon their death. Creating a trust can be deceptively complicated for the do-it-yourselfer, and it can be expensive to have an attorney redo the paperwork. Research whether or not a trust is the best option for your loved one, and if so, hire an attorney to create it.

Most states do not require trusts go through **probate**, which can be time consuming and costly. Probate is the legal process of finalizing anyone's legal presence upon their death. It involves closing out accounts, settling final fiduciary responsibilities, and distributing all possessions, including financial, real property, and more. A person names an **executor** to carry out this process on their behalf, after their death. The executor goes through this process and files it with the state. A trust can establish the decision-making process in advance of a person's death, so that anything within the trust is not part of the probate process. This simplifies the probate process.

If your loved one has just finished the herculean task of making all these decisions, thank them, congratulate them, and celebrate them in some way—they deserve it! If, however, they made decisions a long time ago, they may wish to revisit them.

Here are some situations to consider:

- Are their medical and/or financial power of attorney, executor, and designated guardians still able, willing, and the best choices for these responsibilities?

- Has something in their lives changed that may have affected their suitability?

- Has something changed in your loved one's assets or beneficiaries' lives that they would like to address in their will?

- Maybe someone is no longer in their life, or someone new is—perhaps a new grandchild?

It is a good practice to revisit these decisions periodically, especially after life-changing events such as a wedding, divorce, retirement, a new heir, the death of one of the designees, or the buying or selling of an asset, to make sure the documents still represent their wishes.

Some people make a master file containing all relevant documents and information. We will call it "The File." Many people pull The File out on the same date every year, such as January 1st, or April 15th for review. What types of documents and information are helpful to keep in The File?

Chapter 12

The File

The File is a one-stop-shop for all the information you need to navigate a person's wishes. Having all the details and documents in one place—well before it becomes necessary—can bring a sense of calm and organization to life as well as the dying process.

Like an advance directive, it is helpful to start The File at age eighteen and update it as each new document, item, or account comes into a person's life. If your loved one has that Type A personality that always seems to be one step ahead, this file is probably already done! Though not every item in this list is necessary or appropriate for everyone, it is helpful to give some thought to each item. This file gives your loved one's financial, medical, and legal powers of attorney, as well as their executor, all the information to execute your loved one's end-of-life directives. Though this is a difficult topic to broach for many, it is important for your loved one, their executor, and primary caregiver to have a conversation about the items that need to be organized and to choose where to keep these items. Keep this information together, accessible, and current. Some of these action items require original documents, but much of the information can be stored digitally for easy access and updating.

Here are some items you can help your loved one put together:

- Advance directive

- Financial durable power of attorney

- Will and/or revocable or irrevocable trust with certificate

- Letters to loved ones, loving will, ethical will

- Funeral, burial plot, and mausoleum information, or other internment choices, including insurance to cover these expenses

- Instructions for funeral service, memorial, or celebration of life

- Lawyer's contact information

- Accountant's contact information

- Life insurance policy, agent's name, and contact information

- Medicare, Medicaid, private health insurance, long-term health insurance, account numbers, and contact information

- Birth certificate

- Passport

- Name change documentation

- Adoption papers

- Citizenship papers

- Copies of Social Security card and Medicare card

- Copy of driver's license

- Marriage or divorce certificates

- Military service records

- All accounts at financial institutions, location of safe-deposit box and key

- Real estate mortgage or deed information, homeowners' insurance, property taxes, warranties

- All vehicle titles (car, truck, boat, RV, snowmobiles, etc.), registrations, loans, insurance, and locations

- Investment, retirement, pension, and any other assets or sources of income

- Employment benefits

- Recent tax return, tax accountant, and contact information

- Passwords and login information (phones, computers, tablets, online accounts, etc.)

- Account and contract information (loans, credit cards, lines of credit), co-signers, and authorized users

- Contact information for children, neighbors, other close family and friends, religious contacts

- Location of keys, garage door openers, assets not on the property, i.e., boat, motorhome

That's a lot of paperwork! It falls on the spouse or the executor to handle this after your loved one is gone. Not all of these items apply to every estate. Some of this information may be very difficult to locate without your loved one's help, so it helps to take any steps they can now, before there is an urgent need.

It can take some time to gather, copy, organize, and store this information.

There are several options, including:

- **Paper**: Copy, categorize, and clearly mark each category. Place these documents in a file or envelope. Clearly label and store this file in a fireproof safe at home. You can purchase end-of-life notebooks, binders, and storage containers at stationary stores and online to assist in organizing these items.

- **Digital**: Scan the documents and store digital copies, so that individuals with authority can access them whenever necessary from anywhere with an internet connection. Here are two websites for this:

  - Visit sidedrawer.com for a digital vault service that stores digital copies of documents and assures safety, accessibility, and security. Once the client opens an account and uploads the documents, only people specified in the account information will have access to the files. SideDrawer requires photo identification and a copy of the death certificate for additional authentication.

  - Once the documents are stored, visit theuswillregistry.org to register their location with the U.S. Will Registry. A helpful backup for those who may not know how to access their loved one's files, the U.S. Will Registry gives authorized representatives, with photo identification and a copy of the death certificate, the location where the documents are being digitally stored.

We live in a land of law, lawyers, and paperwork. The goal is to be aware and prepare for the challenges ahead.

Here is a summary of the main steps to help your loved one organize their decisions:

- Advance Directive (living will, medical power of attorney, organ donation)

- POLST

- Do Not Resuscitate

- Financial power of attorney

- Will

- Trusts

- The File

- Recording and safekeeping all documents

A lawyer is not absolutely required to make these choices, but it is usually helpful to have one. The preparations listed here require time and thoughtfulness. This is a difficult task, but it will not get easier with time. It is much easier to complete these tasks before they become urgent.

In addition to these decisions, your loved one may want to choose how they will be laid to rest. Making this plan can ease the emotions surrounding saying goodbye. With many options available, which one is best for your loved one and your family?

Chapter 13
A Final Resting Place

C hoosing a final resting place is an important decision, though it can be a difficult topic. Honoring a person's life is an occasion that deserves full attention and thoughtful planning. This is difficult to achieve while grief-stricken, so it is helpful to plan ahead. Some people want to participate in these decisions about their final resting place, while others only want to address handling the expenses. Every person has the right to choose not to participate. I know people who wanted no part of this discussion; they would pass it off with a humorous comment and let their survivors handle it. Some may already have made decisions; you just need to know the specifics. I know others who made every decision from the flowers, to the casket, burial plot, music, and minister. Some even wrote the program, the menu for the wake, their death notice, and helped with the eulogy! It gave them peace of mind to know their decisions were set, their wishes were known, and they would be honored. To whatever degree your loved one wants or does not want to make decisions, do your best to support them. In chapter 29, we will discuss setting these final arrangements in motion after your loved one's death.

For this stage of the process, there are as many options as there are religions, cultures, traditions, and budgets. In the United States and Canada today, the most common disposition is a "traditional" funeral. This practice is fairly new. It became popular in the early twentieth century, when turning loved ones' remains over to funeral homes became the norm. The "traditional" funeral has no roots in any religion and is rarely practiced outside the United States or Canada.

Traditional Burial

In a traditional burial, the body is usually embalmed and prepared in a mortuary or funeral home. The family may choose to have a viewing before the funeral with the casket present. Traditional funerals are usually held in a funeral home, place of worship, or a venue for a larger gathering. There may also be a graveside service before the casket is entombed in a mausoleum or interred in a cemetery plot. Most cemeteries require a vault for in-ground burials and requirements for the marker. Few of these practices are required by law. You have the right to care for your loved one in a way that is meaningful to them and to you.

Many expenses are involved in a traditional burial. Different options for products affect the price range.

> Visit consumer.ftc.gov for an inventory of different types of charges and the requirements for disclosure by the funeral director.[4]

Today's traditional burial can be the most expensive form of interment. Funeral directors and mortuaries must adhere to certain regulations, assuring the consumer is aware of their options, but the consumer must be aware of the regulations in order for them to be effective. Enforced by the FTC, these regulations are known as the Funeral Rule. Funeral homes are required to offer services and goods à la carte. You may purchase the casket, headstone, grave liner, or vault somewhere other than the funeral home, and the funeral home is required to use them. It is worth shopping around for these items, as well as the cemetery, funeral home, or mortuary. An excellent reference for making funeral arrangements with or without a funeral director is a book by Lisa Carlson, *Caring for the Dead: Your Final Act of Love*. It also includes state-by-state funerary laws, regulations, and dispute resolution information.

Cremation

Cremation is the process of reducing the body to ashes and bone fragments using intense heat, then pulverizing larger bone fragments to a granular texture weighing about five pounds. Cremation provides a wide range of choices. You or your loved one may choose to have the standard body preparation, including embalming. You may rent a casket, have a traditional viewing and funeral service, and then have the cremation performed. Some choose to cremate first, then hold a service with an urn containing the ashes. Others choose what is called a direct cremation, where the body is taken immediately to the mortuary or crematorium and cremated without embalming, viewing, or visitation. The family can receive the remains and decide when they would like to say their final goodbye, in their own time. This is an economical and timely option. Direct cremation works especially well if the family needs to transport the remains to another location in a short amount of time.

Ashes may be placed in a columbarium in a mausoleum within a cemetery. They may also be buried in a regular grave or special section of the cemetery for urns. Some cemeteries allow multiple cremains in a single full-size plot. Others bury the remains on their own land. Some scatter the ashes over an area with special significance for their loved one. If your loved one was in the military or was a military dependent, they may have their ashes scattered at sea free of charge by the Navy or Coast Guard. However, since the ship would be on active duty, the family would not be present for the ceremony. Other options include the family keeping the cremains with them in a container special to their loved one, or dividing the ashes among several vials to give to people closest to the deceased. Ashes can be embedded in stained glass, jewelry, or tattoo ink. Some have celebrated their loved ones with fireworks that contained their ashes. Others have created a memorial garden by planting a special tree or bush in soil amended with their ashes. Consider their passions. One family had their loved one's ashes mixed with concrete and placed to create a reef to support marine life. There are always new ways of memorializing a loved one's cremains. In 2020, more than fifty-six percent of Americans chose cremation over traditional burial. This is expected to increase to eighty percent by 2035. This shift is attributed to costs, environmental concerns, and changing cultural practices.[5]

Green or Natural Burial

These types of burials are becoming more popular, especially with a more environmentally conscientious population. This is a return to the burial practices of mid- nineteenth century America, and a continuation of many Jewish and Muslim burials today. The body is not embalmed, prepared with any toxic materials, or cremated. It is placed in a biodegradable coffin or wrapped in a shroud and interred without a vault. The goal is complete and natural decomposition of the body, allowing it to return to the soil. Over ninety green cemeteries exist in the United States today. Some are specially designated areas within conventional cemeteries. Others are expansive tracts of land, frequently next to an existing protected wildlife or critical habitat area. These designated areas return to their natural state after internment. There are no markers, memorial gardens, or landscaping to indicate a gravesite.[6] If your loved one would like to be buried on rural family property, be sure it is allowed by the local municipality or county, and obtain the required permits. This could be a lengthy process, so start early. Keep in mind, unless you have established a family cemetery on your property, if that property is ever sold, the burial plot is not protected. It may disturbed or repurposed, and you may not have access to it.

> Visit the website Gravematters.us for a preview of Mark Harris' book *Grave Matters: A Journey through the Modern Funeral Industry to a Natural Way of Burial,* an excellent resource for information on cremation, home funerals, and natural burials both at home and in nature. It contains personal stories that provide context to these concepts.

Bio-Cremation (Alkaline Hydrolysis) and Natural Organic Reduction (NOR)

These are two lesser known options for final disposition. They are fairly new and only legal in a few states for human disposition.

Whatever your loved one decides for their final arrangements, they must inform the person who will implement their decisions.

> Visit funerals.org, the Funeral Consumers Alliance for a planning kit called "Before I Go You Should Know," available as a digital download for a small fee.

Just as important as preparing these final decisions, it is important to know how to identify and manage the physical challenges of advancing disease. What can be done to support quality of life?

PART 6

NAVIGATING THE WINDING PATH OF ILLNESS

CHAPTER 14

SYMPTOMS, SIDE-EFFECTS, AND RELIEF

When someone is dying, how do you help them?

Not all of this is intuitive. In fact, most of it is not. The rules for caring for a healthy body go right out the window. A dying person needs a new diet, exercise, sleep routine, and symptom management.

One of our first thoughts may be "What is this going to be like?" There are no certain answers, since everyone experiences serious illness differently. However, you can learn about several common symptoms and situations to give more comfort to your loved one.

Symptom management is a complex topic. You want your loved one to be comfortable.

You need to be able to communicate their discomfort or distress to someone who can help. If they call your attention to a certain symptom, you can determine if it is bothering them enough to call a doctor or the hospice registered nurse, increase their pain medications, or go to the emergency room. To help decide what to do next, if you have hospice, call them. Hospice provides twenty-four hour support to give you guidance.It is important to note, self-medicating without the guidance of a medical provider is usually not a good idea. It is always best to consult a medical professional when taking medication.

If your loved one's symptom comes on suddenly, and it is severe or debilitating, call hospice or a health care provider immediately. If you have difficulty reaching them, you may need to go to the emergency room.

Other symptoms can be chronic. You can determine if their discomfort has been with them for months or longer. This type of discomfort is usually not urgent, and often does not require immediate care. Evenso, chronic discomfort can be exhausting, demoralizing, and very painful. It can affect quality of life in ways those not experiencing it cannot understand. Chronic discomfort can contribute to behaviors that your loved one would not normally show. If you start to feel impatient with your loved one, keep this in mind.

The effectiveness of symptom treatment does not show in test results. Only your loved one knows what is making a difference—what works and what does not. Symptom management must be a joint effort between patient and their health care team, and it requires good communication. Your loved one's health care provider will explain the possible side effects of the pain management treatment, and what a reasonable timeframe is to expect relief. If they do not make this clear, ask them! Doctors do not want your loved one to be uncomfortable. You can help them help your loved one by following instructions, being observant, and immediately communicating any concerns.

Keep a journal to record your loved one's symptoms and care. Record the date, time, and duration of each symptom. Was there anything that made it better or worse, like sitting up, certain positions, or moving around? Has a chronic symptom changed in severity, location, or duration? Getting this information to our health care providers can give them clues to get our loved one comfortable sooner.

Pain

Unmanaged severe pain is usually accompanied by anxiety, fear, difficulty sleeping, reduced appetite, frustration, depression, memories of past pain, anticipation of pain yet to come, and in some cases, thoughts of suicide. When the pain is relieved, those heightened reactions return to their pre-pain state, or go away. Physical changes like bone, nerve, or muscle degeneration can cause chronic pain. The disease itself or side effects from treatments can cause these changes. Because the changes are irreversible, the pain will not go away. The pain must be addressed aggressively on a regular schedule so it does not get out of control. Chronic, unrelieved pain can dominate your loved one's life, making it impossible to focus on what's important to them now. Many tools are available to comfort your loved one. Perhaps most important of all, you can bring compassion, patience, and companionship when they want it.

Not everyone will experience pain. Pain is not synonymous with death. Dying does not cause pain, disease does. Controlling pain is a matter of managing medication and/or nonmedical treatments. Currently, medication is the most effective way to treat serious pain.

How Do They Describe Their Pain?

Describing pain can sometimes be difficult for people. A pain scale is one way to describe how bad the pain feels. The pain scale uses the numbers 0-10 to measure pain, "0" meaning no pain at all, and "10" meaning the worst pain possible. You can also use words like "mild," "moderate," "severe," or "excruciating."

For their health care provider to assist in relieving their pain, your loved one will need to describe the pain they are experiencing. Below are a few words to help describe physical pain. You can ask your loved one what they are feeling and make notes.

- Burning

- Stabbing

- Piercing

- Dull

- Throbbing

- Pinching

- Tenderness

- Aching

- Tingling

- Pressure

- Sharp

- Cramping

If they are already on a prescribed medication, and it is not giving them the pain relief they need, make notes before you call the health care provider. Note what level they describe their pain, and what level was its worst in the previous twenty-four hours. Note what medication they are taking, how often, and what their pain level is one hour after taking their medication. Some patients are reluctant to take their medications as directed because of concerns they have not expressed to their doctor.

Common Myths and Mythbusters
about Pain Management

Myth	Fact
"Using drugs for pain relief will make me an addict."	Hospice patients use opiates for genuine relief from physical pain. Addiction is a known risk, so these drugs must be used only under the supervision of a doctor. It is important for your loved one to share any concerns about addiction, including any personal history of addiction or addiction in their family, with their doctor.
"If I take painkillers now, they will not work for me when I need them later."	One can take oral pain medication for long periods of time before tolerance—the need for more drugs to achieve the same effect—develops. Requiring more medication is most often due to advancing disease rather than tolerance. If your loved one needs stronger relief, their doctor has several options: • Increase the dose or frequency of the medicine. • Add another medication to increase the effectiveness of the primary medication. • Switching to another medication or changing the method of administering it.
"If I take pain medications, I'll be drowsy and out of it."	When beginning regular pain medications, dosage is adjusted for effectiveness. During that fine-tuning, your loved one may be drowsy.
"Opiates like morphine are only offered when death is imminent."	It is not the stage of illness but the degree of pain that dictates which medicine will be used. Treatment starts with a mild medicine at a low dose. If this is not effective, a stronger medicine and/or higher dose is used.

Some patients do not take their medication as prescribed because of its side effects. Most side effects can be controlled or eliminated.

Side Effects of Pain Medication

Medications such as opiates have side effects. Some side effects are pleasant, some unnoticeable, and some bothersome. Bothersome side effects can generally be controlled.

Your loved one may or may not experience these common side effects:

- **Sedation or Drowsiness**: This is typically a temporary side effect of most opiates. Sedation usually subsides in three to five days. Poorly controlled pain is exhausting, so do not confuse sedation with the need to catch up on sleep, once pain is finally relieved.

- **Nausea**: This feeling only lasts a few days. If bothersome, it can generally be controlled with anti-nausea medication. In most cases, anti-nausea medication can be stopped within three to four days, as nausea rarely persists beyond that time. Visit chapter 14 for more information about nausea.

- **Constipation**: Unlike sedation and nausea, this is a chronic side effect of many medications, including opiates. It is also controllable. A mild laxative combined with a stool softener taken on a regular basis can relieve constipation caused by medications. Doctors usually order constipation medications when ordering pain medication. A nurse can recommend dietary modifications to help relieve constipation. Visit chapter 14 for more information about constipation.

- **Confusion, Disorientation, and Cognitive Impairment**: These are among the most feared side effects of opiates. They are not common side effects. Mild cognitive impairment and occasional hallucinations may occur when opiate therapy is started and with significant dose increases. These symptoms will subside within days of regular use. Drowsiness, confusion, and hallucinations can occur during the final days of life, and are not always caused by opiates. Even patients who take no opiates at all may experience this.

It is much easier to anticipate and treat side effects early, rather than wait and have them worsen.

In addition, opiates are very effective in treating not only pain, but also shortness of breath or air hunger. If your loved one is experiencing no pain but having trouble breathing, the same opiates that work for pain may be prescribed to control the shortness of breath. In this case, the dosage may change.

Once the right combination of medicine and dosage is achieved, it is important to not let the pain take over again. Keeping pain away is better than getting it to go away again and again. It is important for your loved one to continue their pain medication at the dose that will keep them comfortable.

Non-Pharmacological Options

Non-pharmacological options can provide comfort and quality of life until medications are needed. They can also complement pharmaceutical treatment.

Here are some treatment options for pain relief:

- Heat and ice

- Acupuncture

- Transcutaneous Electrical Nerve Stimulation (TENS)

- Biofeedback and behavior modification

- Meditation

- Reiki

- Psychotherapy

- Yoga

- Healing touch

- Aroma therapy

- Qi gong

- Herbal teas

- Tai chi

- Guided imagery

- Music

Visit the Resources section for links to websites with guided imagery and calming music.

In addition to specific practices for pain relief, parts of everyday life ease suffering and enhance quality of life.

Here are a few activities to keep in mind:

- **Laughter**: This one is my favorite. Laughter aids in digestion, lowers blood pressure, deepens breathing, and affects mood. Laughter also reduces anxiety, fear, anger, and depression. To bring more laughter into your loved one's life, try a new routine: text or call them with a new joke once a week to make their day—and yours—a little brighter.

- **Music**: Music increases blood flow to the brain, respiration, and muscle strength. Is this a good time to create a playlist or find a favorite musical or concert to watch?

- **Visitors**: Family, friends, or even volunteers from hospice can provide welcome distractions as well as the many other benefits discussed in Chapter One.

- **Relaxation**: Relaxation is the state of relative freedom from anxiety and muscle tension. In addition to music and guided imagery, mindful breathing techniques and massage are very effective. Pet therapy can also be helpful for those who do not have allergies or aversion to animals. Check online to find animal-assisted therapy. When searching online, it is helpful to specify "animal-assisted therapy near me." Without the "near me" in the search request, you will see lots of ads for training support dogs. Check with hospitals, rehabilitation centers, universities, police, and fire departments to see which agencies they use. Police and fire departments both call on animal-assisted therapists to assist victims after traumatic events.

- **Body Massages or Back Rubs**: These relax muscles, increase circulation, and aid sleep.

Shortness of Breath

Shortness of breath is also known as air hunger. For people living with certain diseases such as congestive heart failure, lung cancer, or Chronic

Obstructive Pulmonary Disease (COPD), being on oxygen can be part of everyday life. If breathing becomes labored, supplemental oxygen can relieve the sensation of not getting enough air and the anxiety that comes with this feeling. Anxiety is partly what causes and intensifies this sensation. When our body is no longer functioning enough to support us, supplemental oxygen is no longer effective. It is considered a comfort measure for the patient and their family.

There can be a downside to continuing oxygen. Oxygen is dispensed through a mask or tubes, which can make communicating more difficult, abrade fragile skin, and cause an overall feeling of dryness.

Other methods to relieve air hunger include anti-anxiety medications, opiates, other medications, and holistic practices.

Here are some additional tips for relief:

- Adjust positions, such as sitting up or lying with their head elevated.

- Use a gentle fan to blow across their face, while making sure they do not get chilled.

- Use a humidifier for their room.

- Guided imagery is a relaxation technique where a guide or recording leads a person through calming mental images.

- Use a diffuser or apply essential oils for aromatherapy. Try eucalyptus, citrus, or peppermint.

- Keep them from feeling restricted by loosening clothing and using lightweight blankets.

Nausea

The key to combating nausea is identifying the culprit responsible. Because an issue in one organ can "refer" sensations to another area, it might be difficult to quickly find the underlying cause. This is called **referred pain.** There is a connection between every nerve in our bodies. When we experience something, our nerves send a message to our brain so it can react. The brain then sends a warning, usually in the form of pain, back to the affected area. Sometimes the wires get crossed, and the pain message is sent to an area unrelated to where the issue actually is located in the body. As a result, nausea and other discomforts may not respond to the first remedies. Your loved one's doctor may need to do a little detective work.

In addition to referred pain, nausea can result from one or more of the following:

- Constipation

- Hunger

- Grief

- Medications

- Pain

- Low appetite

- Anxiety

- Chemotherapy

- Infection

- Unpleasant odors

- Unpleasant tastes

- Unpleasant sights

Medications are available for several of these causes. Oncologists commonly prescribe anti-nausea medication for their patient to take before beginning chemotherapy or radiation. Generally, medications are more effective at preventing nausea than relieving nausea once it has taken hold. If medication is not working for your loved one, ask their doctor about changing medication or trying holistic or non-pharmacological options.[1]

If scents or smells are causing nausea, here are some suggestions for possible causes and solutions:

- If the smell of food is bothering your loved one, prepare food in a separate area, or cook outside using a grill. Another option is cooking in a crockpot outside.

- Offer foods that do not need to be cooked, or that can be served cold. Some options are yogurt, frozen fruit, cold sandwiches, smoothies, cheese and crackers, cottage cheese, nuts, and seeds.

- Offer warm foods with little aroma that require less cooking time, such as scrambled eggs, french toast, pancakes, oatmeal, and cream of wheat.

- Use cups with a lid and straw to minimize the scent of beverages.

- Request family and guests to not wear strongly scented toiletries or perfumes while visiting.

- Wash linens and other laundry in unscented detergent and softener.

- Have unscented lotions or moisturizers available.

- Use a fan to provide fresh air or gentle breeze.

Some other ways to alleviate nausea include:

- Have your loved one sit up, or keep the head of their bed raised for at least one hour after eating.

- Loosen clothing.

- Apply a cool compress to their forehead, back of their neck, and wrists.

- Acupuncture is known to help relieve nausea and other discomfort.

- Provide acupressure wrist bands.

- Serve them herbal teas.

Some herbal teas are known to help relieve nausea:[2]

- **Ginger** has been used as a natural nausea remedy for thousands of years. Ginger is used in tablets, chews, candy, and tea.

  ○ To make ginger tea, you can remove the skin with a peeler or leave it on, as the skin is edible and contains nutrients.

  ○ Add one teaspoon of freshly grated ginger root to one cup of boiling water.

- Cover and steep for five to ten minutes.

- Strain and serve.

- **Chamomile** can reduce vomiting frequency. The tea is made from a sweet, earthy flower and has been used to relax digestive muscles.

  - Place one tablespoon of dried chamomile flowers into an infuser and place in a cup.

  - Pour boiling water over the flowers.

  - Steep for five minutes.

- **Peppermint** has a soothing effect on the stomach, especially for nausea related to indigestion.

  - To make tea from fresh mint leaves, you can gently bruise the mint leaves and add them to boiling water.

  - Steep for five to ten minutes.

  - Strain and serve.

- **Lemon** can ease nausea, especially with a little honey.

  - Add one tablespoon lemon juice and half a tablespoon of honey to one cup of boiling water.

  - Let this cool a bit and adjust for sweetness as needed.

- **Cinnamon** is anti-inflammatory and can soothe an upset stomach.

  - To make cinnamon tea, bring three cups of water to boil, then add four cinnamon sticks.

- Simmer for about fifteen minutes.

- Serve warm or hot, and add honey or sugar if desired.

These teas are available in most grocery stores. Experiment with combining some of these teas or adding other herbs.

For an interesting blend, add the following to two cups boiling water:[3]

- Add one teaspoon crushed fennel seeds to reduce gas, bloating, and relax the gastrointestinal tract.

- Add dried lemon verbena for flavor.

- Add one teaspoon grated ginger root.

- Let it simmer for ten minutes.

- Remove from heat and strain through a tea strainer.

- Serve with a squeeze of fresh lemon for added flavor.

Bowel and Bladder Issues

Diarrhea: Loose, watery stool can result from different factors. Contact your loved one's health care team before starting any home remedies or over-the-counter treatments. They may need to change medication or dosage. Other treatments can also contribute to diarrhea, such as chemotherapy. It might be an incontinence problem that calls for ointments and skin care. It is easy to "over medicate" and cause constipation. Diarrhea can cause dehydration, so offer plenty of water, clear broths, electrolyte and fluid replacement drinks, and flat soda. Your loved one's health care team may suggest the BRAT diet (Bananas, Rice, Applesauce, and Toast) to firm up the stools and give a little nourishment. Peppermint, chamomile, or ginger tea may be soothing. Avoid spicy, greasy, or dairy-heavy foods.

It is worth noting, Pepto Bismol does not stop diarrhea. It binds the watery stool and slows it down. Inform the health care team if your loved one's diarrhea does not subside. They may provide medications to help.

Constipation: This means a person is having difficulty passing stool. As nausea is a companion to serious illness, so is constipation. Disease, prescribed medications, dehydration, and immobility can cause constipation. It can cause or worsen pain, fatigue, shortness of breath, and loss of appetite. The sooner it is addressed, the easier it will be to remedy. As with diarrhea, constipation requires a conversation with your health care team for assessment. It is common for those trying to regulate bowels without guidance to find themselves on a pendulum that swings back and forth between constipation and diarrhea. Your health care team may recommend over-the-counter medication, herbal, or non-pharmacological options. Avoid "bulk" or fiber supplements for terminally ill patients. If they do not consume enough water, they can make the problem worse. Non-pharmacological aids include acupressure, acupuncture, and abdominal massage. Encourage whatever physical activity their health care team approves. If possible, avoid long periods of sitting or lying in bed. Herbal aids include warm lemon or lime water, prune juice, high fiber foods, and chewing on fennel seeds.

Use this chart to help identify high fiber foods to aid in digestion:

Constipation - High Fiber Food Chart

In general, people should aim for 25-35 grams of fiber each day.

High Fiber Foods	Serving Size	Dietary Fiber (g)
BREADS AND CEREALS		
Bran Cereal	1/2 Cup	3-13
Popcorn	2 Cups	5
Brown Rice	1/2 Cup	6
Whole Wheat Bread	1 Slice	1-2
Whole Wheat Pasta	1/4 Cup	6
Wheat Bran, Raw	1/4 Cup	6
Quinoa	1/2 Cup	5
LEGUMES		
Kidney Beans	1/2 Cup	8
Navy Beans	1/2 Cup	9
Nuts	1 Ounce	1-3
Lentils	1/2 Cup	8
Black Beans	1/2 Cup	7
Soybeans	1/2 Cup	15
Chickpeas (Garbanzo Beans)	1/2 Cup	6
Lima Beans	1/2 Cup	7
VEGETABLES		
Broccoli	1/2 Cup	4
Brussels Sprouts	1/2 Cup	3
Carrots	1/2 Cup	2
Corn	1/2 Cup	5
Green Beans	1/2 Cup	3
Potato with Skin	1 Medium	4
Sweet Potato with Skin	1 Medium	5
Mixed Vegetables, Frozen	1/2 Cup	4
Artichoke	1 Medium	10
FRUIT		
Apple, with peel	1 Medium	4
Banana	1 Medium	2
Blackberries	1/2 Cup	4
Blueberries	1/2 Cup	2
Pear with skin	1 Medium	5
Prunes	3	3
Orange	1 Medium	3
Raisins	1/4 Cup	3
Strawberries	1 Cup	3

Adapted from "Nutrition for the Person with Cancer During Treatment" A Guide for Patients and Families" (American Cancer Society, 2015) and "Fiber Content of Foods" (Nutrition Care Manual, Academy of Nutrition and Dietetics, 2008)

Bladder Incontinence: This can be caused by weakened pelvic floor or bladder muscles, neurological conditions, medications, and other conditions. There is no cure, but there are options for care and comfort. Your health care team will suggest if catheterization, adult diapers, or other incontinence products are the best solutions. Incontinence can increase the risk of urinary tract infections which require immediate medical attention.

Bladder and bowel problems are common and uncomfortable for those suffering and their caregivers. They are also good examples of topics you will need to become comfortable discussing. If these symptoms are too uncomfortable for the caregiver to handle, it can make it more difficult for your loved one facing these challenges. If you are the primary caregiver, and any of the responsibilities are beyond you, seek assistance from your health care team. They may suggest options for in-home care assistance or guidance on techniques to make the tasks easier. Most hospitals have social workers who can refer you to available services. Visit chapter 7 for more information about this.

Dry Mouth or Thick Saliva

If your loved one is experiencing these symptoms, check with their physician if you suspect an infection. Medication, dehydration, or thrush can cause dry mouth or thick saliva. To help, offer ice chips, chewing gum, frozen fruits like berries or grapes, or fruit ices like melons or peaches.

Drinking papaya juice, club soda, or seltzer water can help thin saliva. Use an over-the-counter saliva substitute such as rinses, sprays, or lozenges. Check with your loved one's health care team to confirm what options are best, considering any concerns for your loved one's ability to swallow. Maintaining good oral hygiene and drinking lots of fluid also helps. Alcohol and tobacco make dry mouth worse.

Dehydration

Decreased consumption of food or liquids and/or excessive loss of fluids are main causes of dehydration. Several symptoms mentioned in this chapter contribute to dehydration, including diarrhea, vomiting, fever, sweating, poor appetite, difficulty swallowing, and anything that causes a person to lose more fluid than they absorb. Dehydration makes it difficult for the body to carry out vital functions and processes. Dehydration is not obvious, so sometimes the signs or symptoms go unnoticed. Keep an eye out for the following symptoms and contact your health care team. Help your loved one prevent discomfort by encouraging them to stay hydrated.

Here are some symptoms of dehydration to watch for:

- Dark yellow or amber colored urine

- Decreased urine output

- Decreased weight

- Dry mouth and sticky saliva

- Sunken, dry eyes

- Confusion

- Thirst

- Constipation

- Changes in heart rate/blood pressure

- Fatigue

- Urinary tract infections

- Headaches

- Muscle cramps

To stave off dehydration, offer plenty of liquids—trying for at least eight to ten cups a day—as well as fruits and vegetables with high water content.[4]

Remember to follow your health care team's guidance. Some of the suggested fruits or vegetables may not be appropriate if they are having digestive issues.

This simple list provides options for hydrating foods and beverages:

Beverages for Hydration

- Water

- Smoothies

- Milk

- Tea

- Soups/broths

- Diluted Juices

- Rehydration beverages(Pedialyte, Liquid IV)

High Water Content Fruits

- Melons

- Apples

- Citrus fruits

- Peaches

- Strawberries

- Kiwi

- Pineapple

- Grapes

High Water Content Vegetables

- Cucumber

- Tomatoes

- Celery

- Lettuce

- Brussel sprouts

- Zucchini

- Broccoli

- Bell Peppers

Skin Problems

Itchiness: Several issues can cause the skin to feel itchy. Skin infections, kidney disease, liver or gallbladder disorders, neuropathy, medication side effects, hallucinations, eczema, and dry skin, also known as xerosis, are the most likely culprits. Our skin is our largest organ and our first defense against infections. Scratching or tearing the skin while trying to get relief from itchiness destroys our protective barrier against microorganisms entering our body. Non-pharmacological options include keeping skin clean without over-washing. Use creams, hydrating gel cleansers, or glycerine soaps. Any cleansers with perfume could be drying. Avoid hot showers or baths that could deplete the natural oils in your skin. Apply moisturizers that do not include alcohol, Alpha-Hydroxy Acid (AHA), or fragrance. Topical and oral medications are also available.

My mother-in-law came to visit during the summer months to escape the Arizona heat for a few weeks. The last few years she visited, our voracious Alaska mosquitoes had no difficulty getting through her rice-paper-thin skin. She did not feel the bites or the blood trickling across her arm. We were concerned that she was unaware of possibly more skin damage. She and I did a quick little inspection and discovered some irritated areas she could not see, caused by her clothing. She changed the style of a few garments and avoided more damage. We also discovered bumping into a cabinet or the dog putting his paw, even gently, on her arm would cause her skin to tear deep enough to make it bleed. Like many elderly, especially on blood thinners or with compromised immune systems, she healed very slowly. This made her vulnerable to infection for a greater length of time. More aware of these frailties, we all took extra precautions—sorry Chewy, no more paw pats—and she was able to avoid infections.

The moral of the story is, you can take small steps to address seemingly minor issues and keep them from becoming major issues.

Skin Irritation and Breakdown: These conditions are likely to occur at some point for everyone. Aging, sun exposure, genetics, and medications are common causes. As a person ages, the decreased collagen and elastin make skin less flexible. Poor circulation can also cause the skin to become fragile and vulnerable. Bedsores are ulcers caused by lying in the same position for too long without moving. Constant pressure on the skin prevents blood flow and causes the skin to break down. Skin frailties are common in the elderly or severely ill before they are bedridden. Neuropathy and diabetes can cause reduced sensation, making it less likely for them to notice wounds or injuries. Make a routine of doing a little inspection. Look for any redness, sores, blisters, or any breaks in the skin that could get infected. Treat and protect these areas. Advise your health care team when you discover infections. It is important to get blood flowing to their entire body. This can help prevent, limit, or repair damage such as bedsores. If your loved one is unable to move around the room, you can help them change position, like rolling from one side to the other, every hour or so. If they are having trouble not keeping a certain position, use a wedge, pillows, or rolled up towels to help stabilize them.

Staying hydrated helps overall skin health and resilience. Applying a moisturizer a couple of times a day helps with elasticity. And, as with itchy skin, use mild moisturizing soaps that will not strip the skin's natural oils. If your loved one is still active, have them wear protective clothing like long-sleeved shirts and long pants to prevent minor skin injuries while enjoying the outdoors. Wide brimmed hats and sunscreen are recommended for protection from sun damage—for all of us!

Change or Loss of Taste

As the body continues its dying process, a person may experience changes in their sense of taste, or even loss of taste. You can help your loved one navigate this by learning about the possible causes of these changes and what foods may balance their new sense of taste.

Mom never had a big appetite, but she ate what she wanted on her own schedule. A couple months after her diagnosis, I noticed she was eating very little. When I offered her food, she would say, "Nothing sounds good right now," or "I'm not really hungry." But one day she said, "Nothing tastes good,"—ding, ding, ding!—we have a winner. Your loved one may be more forthcoming about their eating difficulties, but if they are not, taste could be the culprit.

I had been bringing Mom tiny versions of her favorite foods. She would take a few bites and apologize for not being able to eat more. After she said, "Nothing tastes good," I grilled her on how it tasted to her. She explained that everything tasted metallic, "Like putting your tongue on a screen door." I did not ask how she knew how that tasted!

Although I was trying to entice her with her favorite foods, all I was doing was ruining her memories of what her favorites tasted like. The sad part of the story is, we did not speak up or ask about this symptom. We assumed it was "just part of the deal." We were not with hospice and did not have the support teams in place back then that are available today. So Mom forced down what she could, never to truly enjoy a meal again.

Today, it is typical for a health care team to ask specifically about a patient's appetite and any taste issues, so they can provide possible solutions.

As their health fails, people often lose their appetite. We will discuss this in chapter 8. It is common for people with long-term or end-stage illness to have a dulled sense or loss of taste, or for foods to take on a different taste, such as metallic or bitter. Medications, chemotherapy, and dry mouth can be contributing causes.

Thrush can dull the sense of taste. It's a yeast infection that looks like a thick, white coating on the tongue, and the rest of the mouth and throat, frequently caused by certain medications.[5] If you suspect your loved one has thrush, it is important to get medical advice for proper diagnosis and treatment. The doctor will prescribe the best course of action.

Here are a few non-pharmacological treatments the doctor may add to the treatment plan:

- **Saltwater Rinse**: Dissolve half a teaspoon of table salt in one cup of warm water, swish in the mouth for one to two minutes, then spit it out. The salt has antiseptic properties that soothe and cleanse the mouth.

- **Baking Soda Rinse**: Mix half a teaspoon of baking soda in one cup of warm water, swish in the mouth, and spit it out. Baking soda is a disinfectant.

- **Lemon Juice and Water**: Add the juice of half a lemon to a glass of water and use as a rinse. It is important to note, undiluted lemon juice can cause burning and irritation if applied directly to the lesions.

- **Yogurt**: Because thrush is the result of a yeast imbalance, eating unsweetened yogurt with live and active cultures or probiotics is thought to help correct this imbalance, promoting the growth of healthy bacteria and stopping the growth of thrush. However, eating yogurt does not kill the bacteria that causes thrush.

Anything affecting the mouth, nose, or brain can affect the sense of taste. Changes are unpredictable. Flavors a person previously did not care for can become very tasty, and vice versa.

While your loved one would still like to eat, and while their body is still utilizing nutrition, you can help make eating a more pleasant experience. For people with a diminished sense of taste, using fresh herbs, spices, and seasonings may help. Adding acidic foods like lemons, limes, and oranges help wake up taste buds.

Here are some helpful tips:

- **Food Tastes Bitter**: Add sweet fruits to the meal. You can add honey or maple syrup to foods or drinks. If meat tastes bitter, try serving it cold or at room temperature. Marinated meats may taste less bitter. Try a sweet-and-sour marinade, wine, Italian dressing, or pineapple juice. Bright flavors can make the meal more appetizing. You can also offer blandly prepared chicken, fish, eggs, dairy products, or tofu to add protein to your loved one's diet.

- **Food Tastes Too Sweet**: Add lemon or lime juice, a few drops at a time. Substitute sweet fruits at mealtime with vegetables. Dilute juices or other sweet drinks with water.

- **Food Tastes Too Bland**: Add just a little citrus, like lemon, lime, or orange juice. You can also try vinegar or sea salt.

- **Food Leaves a Metallic Taste**: Be aware of dry mouth, which makes the metallic taste stronger. Add a small amount of healthy fat like a nut butter, avocado, olive oil, and a little sea salt. You can try a squirt of citrus and a small amount of sweetener like maple syrup. Otherwise, try to mask the metallic taste with strong flavors like citrus fruits, sauces, pickles, or other vinegary foods, strong herbs, or spices. Replace metal utensils with ceramic, glass, or plastic.

- **Food Tastes Too Salty**: Add a little lemon juice or vinegar.

Nutritionist Rebecca Katz shares her "Fat, Acid, Salt, Sweet" (F.A.S.S.) technique to make flavor improvements. To enhance or balance flavors, she suggests adding:

> **F**at: Extra virgin olive oil, avocado, or nut butters
> **A**cid: Citrus fruits like lemon, lime, orange, or vinegar
> **S**alt: Sea salt or herbs
> **S**weet: Ripe fruits, honey, or maple syrup

Other issues could affect interest in eating, and there will come a time when nutrition will no longer be a concern.

Until then, here are a few strategies to consider:

- Offer small but frequent meals throughout the day.

- Offer snacks between meals to add protein and calorie intake.

- Shift mealtimes to when your loved one has the most energy, such as mid-morning or afternoon.

- Shift mealtimes to after administering pain medications, when your loved one feels pain-free.

- Use a blender or food processor if your loved one has a hard time swallowing.

- Ice cream, milk shakes, puddings, and custards are good to try, even if only half a cup at a time.

- Serve foods at the temperature your loved one prefers, whether warm, room temperature, or cold. Temperature may affect the taste or texture of foods.

- Protein supplements like Ensure^{TM} or Instant Breakfast^{TM} can serve as an entire meal.

I always added ice cream and fruit, pumping up the calories and adding variety for Mom.

Fatigue

Fatigue becomes a companion to most elderly people and those with serious or terminal illness. Many factors can cause fatigue, such as anemia, depression, insomnia, infections, medications, chemotherapy, and more. Fatigue is the type of tiredness that a good night's sleep will not cure. It is a lack of energy that is not helped by a nap. Nonetheless, conserving and recharging energy can make activities easier or more enjoyable.

Encourage your loved one to engage in an activity that would move their body, if only for a short distance or a few minutes. This might be a walk around the yard, or between rooms in the house. Try chair yoga, tai chi, qi gong, a massage, or acupuncture. Naps will not cure fatigue, but a short nap before and after an activity can provide a little extra vitality to enjoy the event.

At some point, it may become necessary to keep daily activities simple. As with any change in activity level, be sure to consult your health care team. It is important to receive guidance on what a safe level of activity would be for your loved one. Communicate to their health care team about any abrupt changes in energy or awareness.

Some helpful tips for keeping daily activities simple include having your loved one use the bedside commode, especially at night, instead of walking to the bathroom. Have a shower chair available for them to sit while showering. Providing comfort and ease with daily necessities can help your loved one avoid depleting their energy.

Other ideas to help with fatigue include pet therapy. If your doctor agrees there are no issues that would prohibit animal assisted therapy, the hormones released while interacting with friendly animals can relax and help with stress, which may relieve fatigue. Additionally, some people use essential oils like citrus, peppermint, or rosemary as aromatherapy to energize them. As always, keeping your loved one well hydrated is essential. Medications are also available. These seem like small measures, but they may give just enough energy for the next activity.

Eating balanced meals—even if very small—that include protein and fiber can stabilize blood sugar, which gives energy. Consult a dietician about protein and calorie needs and revisit as conditions change.

Here is a list of foods to increase proteins or calories:[6]

Increasing Calories & Protein

How to Increase Calories

Try adding these calorie-dense foods to soups, sauces, entrees, desserts, snacks, or beverages:

- Avocado
- Butter
- Cheese
- Coconut milk
- Cream cheese
- Dried fruit
- Eggs
- Granola
- Honey
- Ice cream
- Jam
- Margarine/vegetable oil spreads
- Mayonnaise
- Olives
- Oils (olive, avocado, canola, coconut, etc.)
- Peanut butter
- Powdered milk
- Salad dressing
- Nuts and seeds
- Sour cream
- Whipped cream
- Whole milk

How to Increase Protein

Try adding these protein-dense foods to soups, sauces, entrees, desserts or beverages:

- Beans
- Bone broth
- Cheese
- Cottage cheese
- Eggs
- Frozen yogurt
- Fish and shellfish
- Instant dry milk
- Instant breakfast powders
- Lentils
- Meat/game/poultry
- Milk
- Nut butters
- Nuts and seeds
- Oral nutrition supplements (Boost, Ensure, etc.)
- Protein powder
- Peas
- Quinoa
- Tofu, tempeh, or edamame
- Wheat germ
- Yogurt

Visit the resources section for a link to download the calories and protein chart.

Delirium

Also known as confusion, delirium is a serious change in mental abilities that comes on quickly, within a few hours or days. Many issues can cause delirium, such as long or severe illness, neurological conditions, insomnia, uncontrolled pain, imbalance in the body, such as low sodium or calcium, infection, surgery, medications, drug or alcohol use, or withdrawal. Symptoms may come and go during the day, but they tend to worsen at night, sometimes known as sundowning. Delirium is common in hospitals, especially ICUs, and long-term care facilities.

The symptoms of delirium look similar to dementia. The patient may have both conditions. Informing their health care team when these symptoms first appear can make a difference in their ability to calm the symptoms. Some symptoms seem fairly commonplace, as most of us can get easily distracted or occasionally have trouble focusing. Below is a list of symptoms of delirium from the Mayo Clinic.[7]

If you see any of these symptoms of delirium in your loved one, contact their health care team:

Reduced Awareness of Surroundings:

- Trouble focusing on a topic or changing topics

- Getting stuck on an idea rather than responding to questions

- Being easily distracted

- Being withdrawn, with little or no activity, or little response to surroundings

Poor Thinking Skills:

- Poor memory, such as forgetting recent events

- Not knowing where they are or who they are

- Trouble with speech or recalling words

- Rambling or nonsense speech

- Trouble reading or writing

Behavioral and Emotional Changes:

- Anxiety, fear, or distrust of others

- Depression

- A short temper or anger

- A sense of feeling elated

- A lack of interest and emotion

- Quick changes in mood

- Personality changes

- Seeing things that others do not see

- Being restless, anxious, or combative

- Calling out, moaning, or making other sounds

- Being quiet and withdrawn

- Slowed movement or being sluggish

- Changes in sleep habits

There are things you can do that may lessen the symptoms of delirium. If your loved one seems disoriented, gently assisting them to become more aware and engaged can help maintain their stability.

It can be particularly confusing for them if they have reversed their sleep cycle. To help gradually shift their sleep cycle, plan a more active daytime schedule that includes moving around and visits from family or friends. Discourage naps. Providing natural sunlight, a bedroom with a window, and a clock within view can help bring consistency to their sleep schedule. Staying well hydrated can help regulate their sleep. Encourage conversation. Talk about things and people they know: how their day or night was, who has visited, who is coming to see them—anything familiar and non-confrontational. If they seem to grow agitated, change the subject. The idea is to orient them to where they are and what time it is, and to engage them in current events. Have comfortable, familiar items around them: pictures, a favorite blanket, or a piece of memorabilia. Be sure they have access to their glasses or hearing aids, if it is safe to do so. On days they seem more confused, or their reality seems different from yours, it is okay. If your efforts to reorient them did not work that day, do not blame yourself. This *is* their reality—that day. If they are simply confused—not agitated, scared, hallucinating, or in danger of hurting themselves or others—let it go. It is not important that you convince them you are right. In fact, this can do more harm than good.

"What difference does it make that Mom thinks it's Tuesday?"—wash, rinse, repeat. The rehash of an old, fruitless discussion between siblings that never ended well. Of my two siblings that split Mom's care when I was not with her, one of them truly believed that all conversations with Mom must be completely factual and accurate, and that she be engaged at all times. They thought this would keep her from getting more confused. If this sibling was with Mom when I arrived, I would either hear their frustrating "discussions" firsthand, or my sibling would recount their version of these conversations. They would not let it go.

The most difficult part of watching Mom's disease progress was witnessing the intermittent symptoms of delirium that came closer to the end. I have heard other people's recollections of their loved one's severe delirium symptoms, so I know how fortunate we were to only experience this intermittent level of delirium. For me, the worst were the personality changes and memory issues. It was like I was losing my mom before she was gone. This vibrant, independent, self-assured woman would turn into an insecure shadow of herself.

At times she felt overwhelmed by her fear of doing something that would cause us to not love her or want to be with her. In the first instance, she called me to her room, where I found her crying. My mom was not known to cry. That was my first sign something was not right. She asked if my husband Greg would forgive her for forgetting his birthday the week before. His birthday was months before. I lied. I told her she did not forget; she had me get him new driving gloves that he loves. She did not challenge my story. She did not acknowledge that she did not recall my version of events. She just seemed relieved. Mom and Greg had a wonderful relationship that she knew could never be marred by anything like that. On the surface, this sounds like a minor instance. But it was such a departure from the mom I knew. The memory lapses became a little more frequent, but the topics were inconsequential—until one day that still brings tears.

A visitor had started talking about their plans for the holiday season coming up—something Mom was not aware of at that time. After they left, Mom asked what my plans were. I told her we were keeping it low key. Greg and our son Jamie would stay home, and I would be with Mom. She got very upset and said she did not want me away from them for Christmas; she wanted me at home with them. I eventually agreed, thinking I would have the other siblings split my time. But that was not what she was thinking. Mom wanted to fly to Anchorage and spend the holiday with us. She was not physically able to handle a trip like this, and she knew that. So we thought. The trip would be difficult enough for someone who was in bed much of the time, weak and sometimes unstable from pain meds. But our home was a tri-level. No matter what, there would be stairs to navigate, which was not something she was capable of doing at this point. I felt concerned about how she would respond to me saying it would not work.

Trying to not be too heavy handed, I just told her that probably was not a good idea. She was genuinely surprised. Rarely did I disagree with her ideas, and never before about her coming to be with us. The look of surprise turned to hurt, her eyes teared up, and she quietly asked why. I could count on one hand the number of times I had seen a look of vulnerability or hurt on my mom's face. It was painful to see. I just wanted to make her understand and be okay with it. I explained that she was not strong enough to take that long flight or to go up and down our stairs. I told her we could take her medications and equipment, but I was concerned about her being so far away from her doctor. As tears slid down her cheeks, the conversation seemed to be over. I kissed her good night and went to bed thinking about how dejected she looked. My mind raced, trying to figure out which decision I needed to reverse to fix this.

The next morning, still unsure of how to fix this, I was caught off guard again. A chipper Mom started our day saying, "It occurred to me, Christmas is next week isn't it? I'd like to come up to Anchorage and spend a few weeks with you. How does that sound?"

Dumbfounded that we were back at square one with this discussion, I was trying to think fast before the delay became obvious and awkward. Which decision do I walk back? How can I make this okay and not hurt? I decided to be more definite. In a gentle but slightly more assertive tone, I told Mom we had discussed it the night before and decided it cannot be done. Again, she asked why. I explained cancer had taken too much of her—she was not strong enough, it would take her life even faster, and I would not help it along. Her tears were streaming, and with quiet sobs she said, "I won't be any trouble. I'll take care of myself."

This was not my mom. This was not the young woman that took an idling locomotive for a joy ride, played—and won—poker with high rollers in after-hours clubs, who raised two young children as a widow and solved everyone else's problems. But it *was* still her. And now I had to be the strong one.

If your loved one is suffering from delirium, and exhibiting any of the symptoms above, remember, they are still the same person who they were before, even though they have no control over their behavior, thought processes, or emotions.

Mom was home. She was safe, comfortable, and cared for by her children, but I still felt guilty. Knowing what's best and doing what's right still did not spare us that feeling. We just had to make the best of it.

> **To Wrap It Up**: Symptoms of illness, side effects of treatments, and age-related decline affect each person uniquely. Individuals will have varying levels of relief from different protocols. Discuss all pharmaceutical, non-pharmacological, naturopathic, and holistic approaches with the health care team, always with an eye towards new information that leads to quality of life.

Symptoms may arise that require professional medical care beyond what you can provide at home. If this happens, a hospital stay may be necessary. Hospital stays are very common for patients with a terminal diagnosis, though they are not inevitable. If your loved one is admitted to the hospital, communication is key to helping them receive the care they need and protecting them from processes they do not need. How do you navigate the complex world of hospitals?

PART 7

MAKING THE BEST OF A HOSPITAL STAY

CHAPTER 15

THE IMPORTANCE OF CLEAR COMMUNICATION

E veryone reacts differently when they face the decision to go to the hospital. Some may want to go, anxious to have their distress relieved. Some may be adamant about *not* going, for any number of reasons. In any case, if your loved one must stay in the hospital for more than a few days, you can make it more comfortable for them—and help yourself feel better too.

This is a good time to make sure you are clear about DNRs, POLSTs, hospice care, and the need to go to the hospital. Choosing to not be resuscitated, or to not receive curative medical treatment, does not mean refusing all medical care. These orders do not mean refusing treatment for severe symptoms or issues unrelated to their terminal illness. Everyone has the right to not be in pain or suffer unnecessarily at the end of their life. If this cannot be accomplished at home, a hospital stay or inpatient hospice may be needed to get things under control.

If your loved one is in hospice care, anytime there is an issue or level of discomfort that you feel needs medical attention or a trip to the hospital, contact the hospice nurse first. Chapter 23 explains the reasons for this.

Once at the hospital, your loved one will be seen first by a triage nurse and eventually a doctor. Before you get too far down the hospital protocol trail, be sure your loved one clearly communicates their diagnosis and care goals. This can be a shortcut through an exhausting system.

The nurse or doctor will ask if your loved one has an advance directive. In 1990, the Federal Patient Self-Determination Act was passed, requiring all health care institutions receiving Medicare funds to inform their patients of their rights to accept or refuse care and to create advance directives for their care.

If your loved one wants to return home as soon as possible, and their health care team knows their comfort care goals, the team can focus on what is important to your loved one. They may be able to address the issue and help them get home sooner.

The goal of doctors and hospitals, especially emergency departments, is to "fix" issues. To accomplish this, the process typically involves examining, testing, questioning, evaluating, sometimes hospitalizing, diagnosing, and so on. All these steps serve the purpose of getting to the big picture. But you already know what the picture is, and it cannot be "fixed." Knowing this, the goal is relief. In order to get relief, there will have to be some examinations. If you share what you know and explain your loved one is on a treatment protocol, or if they are on comfort care only, this will possibly spare them unwanted time and procedures in the hospital.

However, it does not always work this way. Sometimes it is best to stay in the hospital. Per the American Medical Association (AMA), patients of sound mind who are not in danger of hurting themselves or others have the right to refuse treatment and leave the hospital against medical orders. But if the doctor strongly suggests they stay, it is not because they are trying to fill hospital beds. Take the doctor seriously.

When a short emergency room visit turns into a hospital stay, the key to reducing stress and providing comfort is knowledge of how you can make it the best possible experience. Hospital stays will never be luxury hotel visits, though the health care team does try to comfort patients—and serves those fantastic hospital meals in bed. Aspects of a hospital stay can be uncomfortable. In many cases, those things are necessary to meet the goal of providing the best possible care. Having said that—making the best of this experience puts the ball in your court more often than you might think.

Clear communication is the most important tool to make your loved one's hospital stay the best it can be. Yet clear communication is not always as simple as it sounds. When your loved one is first admitted, certain obstacles can inhibit expressing what they need and want. Here are some stumbling blocks that, with awareness, you can help your loved one overcome.

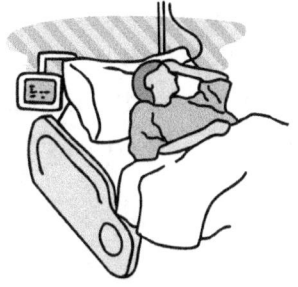 First, it is helpful to be aware of your loved one's ability or desire to communicate. They may feel distress about needing to go to the hospital. They may have been given medication to make them comfortable, but this medication may cloud their thinking. Additionally, the process of triage can be exhausting. Triage is the process by which patients are evaluated and prioritized as they wait to be seen, based on the urgency of their medical condition. Your loved one will wait to be assigned a room. Once their room is assigned, they will settle in, possibly undergo initial testing and treatments, and receive a doctor's evaluation. This process often takes time, and the long hours can leave your loved one too tired to communicate effectively.

Second, when your loved one has no familiarity, relationship, or history of trust with the new health care team, this can be a barrier to clear communication. In seventy percent of U.S. hospitals today, once patients are admitted, the physician overseeing all of their care will be a hospital staff doctor, called a **hospitalist**, not their primary care physician.[1]

In this model of health care, hospitalists are physicians whose entire practice is caring for patients during their hospital stay. They do not have patients, clinics, or offices outside the hospital. They provide the same level of care that your loved one's primary care physician provides outside the hospital. Because hospitalists rotate departments, your loved one may see more than one doctor during their stay. The hospitalist model helps meet the increasing demand for physicians for outpatient care. The upside for hospitalized patients is, hospitalists stay onsite for the duration of their shift. This provides greater access and faster responses. The downside is, your loved one may not feel as comfortable communicating with doctors they do not know as well as their primary care physician.

To help your loved one communicate with medical professionals, it is highly recommended to have someone accompany them to any medical appointments. It can help them feel at ease, knowing they have someone familiar—you, a friend, or other family member—in their corner. If possible, it is helpful to have a **health care advocate** present as a second set of ears for questions and answers.

Mom and I would discuss her questions and concerns in the days leading up to her next treatment. I would write them down and give her the list to take to her appointment. I also made sure to accompany her. Occasionally, when we would talk about the appointment later, I would recall some of the conversation differently. When this happened, I would call the doctor for clarification. Having an extra pair of ears went a long way to ease our anxiety.

Having a health care advocate streamlines communication. This is typically someone in your family. The health care team can discuss treatment plans, updates, and changes in your loved one's condition with the advocate, who acts as the liaison for the rest of the family. Effective communication between your loved one, their advocate, the doctor, and health care team builds trust and strengthens working relationships.

Early in the admitting process, your loved one will be asked about their current medications, advance directive, and POLST. This is to confirm the information stored in their **Electronic Health Records (EHRs)**, a digital version of a patient's chart available to authorized users. Though most medical facilities participate in this system, it is helpful to keep your own list of current medications and copies of the directives. Some patients or caregivers bring all their medications to the hospital, in case the written schedule of meds is not immediately available. However, once admitted, use of a patient's own medications is discouraged for safety reasons. Generally, hospitals have a policy against using them.

Hospital stays may be an important part of your loved one's care. Ask the doctor if they expect your loved one to be in the hospital more than a few days. If so, how can you make their stay feel more like home?

CHAPTER 16
COMFORTS OF HOME

A way from the familiar surroundings of home, staying in the hospital can feel lonely, sterile, or unfamiliar. Yet a longer hospital stay may be the safest place for your loved one as they receive certain treatments or care. Learning how to make a hospital stay more pleasant can have a positive impact on how your loved one feels and responds to treatment.

You can help your loved one's hospital stay be more comfortable by utilizing these hospital hints:

- **Bring a Few Things from Home:**

  - Your loved one's favorite pillow, blanket, and/or something familiar they associate with being relaxed

  - Their personal toiletries, such as toothpaste, hair care products, and their favorite moisturizer

  - Cell phone and charger for staying in touch with calls, messages, or video chats to help them feel connected

  - Favorite photos of loved ones, friends, pets, locations, or events

  - Comfortable clothing like a favorite robe, pajamas, slippers, underwear

- A device to watch movies, listen to music, and read ebooks, with headphones

- A sleep mask and ear plugs give relief from the lights and sounds of a working hospital

- Favorite food or snacks. This is especially helpful if your loved one is having taste and flavor issues you know how to work with! Bring their favorite takeout for both of you to share on a dinner date. Even if they do not feel like eating much, thoughtfulness and companionship are comforting.. **Check with their doctor about any dietary restrictions.** Be sure to put your loved one's name on anything brought in for them. Hospitals are busy places, and things can get misplaced.

- **Find Your Personal Advocate or Staff Connection**: Just as it is more efficient for the doctor to communicate with just one or two people, it helps to identify someone on the care team to be the point person with whom you communicate. This could be the particular nurse, aid, or medical student you see most often. This could also be your loved one's **case worker**. Many hospitals assign case workers to every patient admitted. Case workers help coordinate ongoing care with the health care team and aid communication between specialists. They assist with other aspects of care that can differ slightly at each hospital. In many hospitals, this person helps determine the support needed, forms a discharge plan, and handles the referrals to services needed after discharge. Your loved one can expect a visit from their case worker early in their stay. If your loved one is in hospice, some programs have their version of a caseworker who helps coordinate care. Our inclination is to ask a question or make a request of the first person who enters the room. This does not always work. If it doesn't, ask your point person. Certain requests may have to go up the food chain, but your point person is likely to follow through.

- **Ask for Less**: This is something most people are not aware they can do. Some of these requests may not be granted, or not granted right away, if they require a doctor's approval. Nevertheless, you can always ask, especially if you think something will make your loved one more comfortable.

- **Check Vital Signs Less Frequently**: Unless your loved one is in the Intensive Care Unit (ICU) or otherwise requiring close monitoring, it may not be necessary to have their vital signs checked while they try to sleep through the night. It is worth asking the doctor if this can be paused overnight.

- **Request Silent Alarms**: Machines that administer medications and monitor vital signs may have alarms that can be silenced in the room. Ask the nurses to switch them off if station monitoring is available.

- **Request Fewer Interruptions During the Day**: Rest or quiet time with a loved one are difficult to come by in a hospital building that can feel like a self-contained city. Ask to have their room door closed. If they are in a shared room, consult their roommate before requesting to close the door. If they are in a private room, ask the nurse to post a note on the door requesting all visitors to check with the nurses' station before entering. This would not apply to doctors making rounds, nor would it work in an ICU, where accessibility must be efficient. But if this is possible for your loved one's room, it will calm some of the traffic.

- **Request Fewer Blood Draws**: At a certain point, there is no need to analyze blood anymore, but the order may still be in the chart.

Ask the doctor if this and any other ongoing procedures can be removed from the standing orders.

- **Request a Fan**: Most hospitals have them available upon request. They help with air circulation and provide white noise to cover hospital noise. This can help people with anxiety. For those with slight breathing issues, the slight breeze from a fan can aid breathing.

- **Request Anti-anxiety or Pain Medication**: If your loved one is scheduled for a procedure that they are extremely anxious about, ask the nurse for medication beforehand to help with anxiety or pain.

- **Request Help with Staying Mobile**: Doctors will often have standing orders to keep their patients as ambulatory as possible. If your loved one has this standing order, and nurses do not assist them to move as much as they can, there may be a reason—especially if your loved one is too weak or uncomfortable. In any case, ask for help with movement, however possible. Immobility leads to loss of strength. It can be as much as a walk around the nurses' station or as little as getting to a chair and sitting up for a while. Just as staying active at home is important, so it is while in the hospital. It keeps systems working better, can help with pain, and it feels so good to go back to bed!

In addition to bringing familiar items that help a hospital stay feel more like home, you can help create a comfortable environment in the hospital by building bonds with the health care team caring for your loved one. How do you connect with these people and create mutually trusting relationships?

CHAPTER 17

COLLABORATING FOR CARE: STRENGTHENING PROVIDER CONNECTIONS

O ne of the most important aspects of medical care is the relationship between a patient and the people caring for them. The building blocks of relationships with nurses and doctors are the same as other important relationships in life. There must be trust, open communication, respectful interaction, active participation, and feedback.

It often feels easier to talk about the delicate details of symptoms with the doctor or nurse practitioner one has been seeing for years. A longstanding relationship has established trust and care; there is no embarrassment or fear of judgment in conversations. Now your loved one must start over at a time when they may feel uncomfortable, unsure, and possibly scared. It takes participation by the patient and provider to build a relationship that creates the best possible outcome.

It takes time, but it can happen with the following keys:

- **Open Communication**: This means expressing concerns, needs, and preferences openly. It helps the health care team understand unique situations and builds trust. Patients often hide symptoms because they do not want to tell. Their nurse might miss the indicators or forget to ask. Some believe certain issues can wait until the doctor returns. Not necessarily so. Let the nurse know what is going on. They may be able to address a new concern immediately, or they can contact the doctor instead of waiting for rounds. Sometimes it takes a while to get a response from the doctor, unless it's urgent. The sooner you communicate, the sooner they can help.

- **Respectful Interaction**: Treating the health care team with respect and kindness helps build a trusting relationship. It goes a long way to acknowledge them when they enter the room, remember their names, and show the same consideration to the entire team. These are the types of things that foster mutual respect—and they just might make a small difference in the level of warmth or attentiveness in your loved one's care. Human nature plays a role, even for the most dedicated workers. Frankly, would you want to spend more time than necessary with someone who is surly and demanding every time you meet them?

Part of showing respect is keeping personal "expert opinions" in check. Online research and anecdotal stories do not give someone any kind of expertise. They can give you enough information to ask more specific questions, but beware of crossing that fine line between asking and challenging. Be prepared for answers that do not match your expectations. Keep in mind, the things you might find objectionable may not be in their power to change—like the food. There has probably never been a nurse who has not been chewed out about the food. Do not complain—they did not prepare it.

Mom had several short stays in the hospital during her illness, lasting about three or four days. She would often be admitted shortly before my return from Anchorage. I would finish my shift at work and head to the airport. My flight would always arrive around nine o'clock at night. I would take a cab to Mom's, get her car, and head to the hospital. I never had a nurse tell me I was too late to come sit with her, or tell me when I had to leave.

They would offer me a soft drink or water when they came to check on her. Whenever I would leave Mom's room during a procedure, they would offer a seat at the nurses' station. I never assumed any privilege and appreciated the exceptions. I asked questions without a challenging tone. I was careful not to insinuate any expertise. I would introduce myself and make a point to use their names. I would bring in treats after dinner or muffins for the morning shift. They knew me, and they knew I was there for Mom. They went out of their way to communicate with me. They would tell me if the doctor had made his rounds before I arrived, or if any of his orders changed. These were small things, but they were important to me. None of this was difficult; it seemed natural. When you are worried about your loved one, making conscious efforts to build relationships with the people caring for them can help ease your fears.

- **Following Treatment Plans**: Being a little lax in following doctors' orders outside the hospital may or may not have contributed to this hospital stay. In any case, being a willing—even if not enthusiastic—participant in the treatment plan shows the health care team you are willing to work with them. This will garner their respect.

- **Patience**: Yes, even the patient—and their family—must practice patience. At any time, emergencies can throw schedules off. In the hospital, a schedule is a plan, but the plan can be overridden without notice. Do not take it personally when a test or procedure is rescheduled, a doctor visit is delayed, or medication is a little late. It is almost always because someone is having a worse day than your loved one.

One of the more unpredictable schedules can be the doctor's visits, also called rounds. Most doctors have a routine they follow for each aspect of their practice. It is common for them to see their hospitalized patients early in the morning. They sometimes return for evening rounds. If your loved one is in a hospital that utilizes hospitalists, they also have routines. Their number of patients and each patient's status can limit their time with each patient. Another factor is how much time the patient or family "needs" with the doctor. This is unpredictable and can change the schedule. During rounds, some patients do not need more than the minimum amount of time with their doctor, while others want all the time they can get.

While doctors with a good bedside manner try to give all the time their patients want, it is not always possible. This may come off as being less than completely attentive. If you can keep in mind they may still have fifteen patients to visit in varying stages of illness, it is easier to accept the need to keep your time with them efficient. It is helpful to write down your concerns in advance. Limit your questions to three or four. Try to keep pleasant conversation, anecdotes, and questions to a ten to fifteen minute visit. Always keep in mind, your loved one can ask the nurse to contact the doctor at any time with questions or concerns, if they do not feel comfortable waiting until the next rounds. They might get the on-call doctor or a hospitalist who just rotated into the schedule. They may be unfamiliar with your loved one, but they are available.

To Wrap It Up: Hospital stays can be more comfortable with preparation and human connection. You can do much to help your loved one have an easier time in a challenging situation away from home.

Utilize these helpful hints for a comfortable hospital stay:

- Unless a medical event is urgent and you have called EMTs, call your loved one's health care team before deciding to go to the hospital. At the first opportunity, provide their list of medications, POLST, DNR, diagnosis, and care goals.

- Be patient. Being evaluated and admitted will likely take much longer than is comfortable.

- Be an advocate for your loved one if you are their health care agent.

- Bring comfort items from home and request accommodations like quieter alarms or less night vital signs checks if possible.

- Build a relationship with the new health care team by being open and honest, and by communicating with kindness and respect.

If your loved one is in the hospital, it is because a medical professional thinks that it is the best place to provide the level of care they need right now. It is not uncommon for people with terminal illnesses to be admitted to the hospital at least a few times in the course of their illness. The hospital will stabilize the issue that brought them there, but they can return home with anxiety, anger, depression, or spiritual concerns. What can be done to comfort the heart, mind, and soul?

PART 8

UNDERSTANDING AND CALMING THE STRESS OF THIS NEW REALITY

CHAPTER 18
EMOTIONS

This experience will challenge the coping skills of your loved one and everyone close to them, including you. Each person reacts uniquely to the experience of coming to the end of life. The fears, anxieties, and myriad of emotions are quite different for your loved one than they would be for you. It can feel uncomfortable to be present at the end of someone's life because it can be difficult to relate to what they are feeling.

Every emotion your loved one will feel is powerful and affects the quality of their life. On difficult days, they may want to talk about their fears, concerns, or regrets. Do not be offended if you are not the person in whom they confide. If they open up to you, remember to give them a judgement-free zone. This is where you can listen respectfully to things that may be hard to hear. Do not dismiss their fears as silly or unfounded. Always keep their confidence.

Being aware of common emotions—and what helps people through them—provides insight to help your loved one have the best possible experience.

Fear

Fear is sometimes the first emotion a person feels when they learn they are dying. Even people with strong spiritual beliefs can experience fear. When will it happen, how long will it take, what will it be like, and for some—what will happen to them or their soul when they die? Fear can feel very powerful.

By helping your loved one feel like they can share their fears, you can comfort them as a supportive, loving listener. You can help them find answers to their questions whenever possible.

Depression

Depression is more than sadness. It can bring changes, including loss of interest in nearly all activities, loss of appetite, altered sleeping habits, difficulty in concentrating or decision making, little interest in talking, decreased energy, feelings of guilt, hopelessness, or worthlessness. In serious cases, there may be thoughts of suicide. Depression can be caused by sustained anxiety, fear, or unmanaged pain. If your loved one is taking medications and experiencing depression, their doctor may review their prescriptions. Some medications cause depressed moods. Some of these symptoms can be part of the natural dying process, so it may be difficult to tell if depression is the cause. Depression is not always present in dying patients. If you feel your loved one is suffering from depression, contact their doctor or nurse.

Grief

For those approaching the end of life, it is normal to grieve multiple losses. They may grieve the loss of their functions and abilities, as well as who and what they will leave behind. They may mourn the loss of people who do not know how to be part of this chapter in their life. If you sense your loved one is grieving, ask them if they would like to share their feelings with you.

They may be comforted by a visit from their spiritual leader or a counselor.

Anxiety

Anxiety is normal for anyone with a life-limiting illness. They may feel anxious about unfinished business, unresolved conflicts, care of dependent survivors, or changing roles in the family. Anxiety can come from worrying about medical expenses or changes in their body. These and other issues may loom large in the beginning of this journey, but they will eventually resolve or fade into the background. Until then, you can be there to help.

What does anxiety look like?

Take note if you or your loved one are experiencing the following symptoms:

- A Feeling of Panic

- Feeling as though they are losing control

- Difficulty solving problems

- Feeling excitable

- Feeling angry or irritated

- Increased muscle tension

- Trembling and shaking

- Headaches, upset stomach, diarrhea, constipation

- Sweaty palms, racing pulse, difficulty breathing

- Problems sleeping

- Difficulty eating

What helps with anxiety?

Non-pharmacological solutions can be very helpful if introduced before anxiety becomes chronic. If your loved one is unable to eat, sleep, or recover from acute anxiety with coping techniques, contact their health care team. Medication can help.

Experiment with the following tips:

- **Peaceful Environment**: Soothing music, or music in their favorite genre, can be comforting. Continuous bright lights and loud noises can cause stress. The everyday chaos of normal life—like kids and pets running through the room—can now overload your loved one's senses.

- **Gentle Touch**: Holding their hand, or a back or foot rub, can soothe their nerves.

- **Deep Breathing Exercises**: Breath is key to relaxing the body and mind.

Visit the Resources section for a link to the article "10 Useful Breathing Techniques to Try Anywhere."[1]

- You can guide your loved one through this simple technique:

  - Slowly inhale through the nose for a count of five.

  - Hold the breath in for a few seconds.

  - Release the breath through the nose for a count of five.

  - Picture a place that is calming and relaxing.

  - Repeat for five minutes.

Visit the Resources section for a link to sixteen minutes of guided imagery, called "English Garden."

- **Listening to Music**: Music lowers production of the stress hormone cortisol, helping with stress. Happy tunes are mood enhancers. For calming and help with sleep, choose music that plays about sixty beats per minute. This tempo encourages alpha brain waves associated with relaxation. Calming music can also lower blood pressure and heart rate.[2]

Visit the Resources section for a link to a video that provides several hours of soothing music.

- **Gratitude**: Help your loved one refocus on positive aspects of life. Talk with them and intentionally focus on things and people they are grateful for—whatever brings them joy.

- **Spirituality and Prayer**: Your loved one may contemplate the meaning of their life. If you share their beliefs, they may ask you to pray with them. Some people, especially at this unsettling time, struggle with their spirituality. Talking with someone from their religious community may provide solace. Reading religious texts or listening to religious music may be comforting. If they are not part of a specific religious community but would like to speak to someone, hospitals and hospice teams have chaplains trained to help people of all faiths and spiritual backgrounds.

- **Humor**: Laughter is an integral part of life! Not everyone may see humor in dying. But if your loved one has a sense of humor, it is important to allow them to feel it. If humor feels inappropriate during a solemn time, it is a worse tragedy to deny them such a pleasurable part of life. "Reading the room" is important, but there may be the right time for a good laugh. For those still not convinced it's okay to bring out the joke book or their favorite comedy routine—there is a physiological benefit to laughter. Laughter stimulates the release of endorphins, hormones that reduce stress and anxiety. It also triggers the release of dopamine, a neurotransmitter associated with the feelings of reward or pleasure.

- **Journaling**: From a scientific standpoint, while stress activates the "fight-or-flight" response in the sympathetic nervous system, journaling activates the "rest-and-digest" response of the parasympathetic system. Meaning, it is calming. It regulates breathing, blood pressure, and heart rate, which helps one think more clearly. The health benefits of journaling have been scientifically proven over the last few decades, including decreased pain, strengthened immune system response, and improved ability to cope with illness.[3] Journaling is accessible anytime, anywhere with just paper and pen. Some may prefer their computer, or a voice memo on their phone. Journaling is a good option for those with mobility issues who cannot utilize more physical stress management like exercising or walking. If your loved one already journals, encourage it. If it is new to them, you can find great articles online with ideas on how to start. There is no wrong way to journal—just suggestions on how to get the most out of it.

Visit the Resources section for the link to a helpful article written by Elizabeth Scott, PhD., "Why You Should Keep a Stress Relief Journal," that details the benefits of different types of journaling.

- **Talking**: Ask your loved one if they want to talk about specific concerns they have. Sometimes they just need to talk and be heard. In a handbook created by one of our local hospice groups with contributions from doctors, clinicians, chaplins, social workers, nutritionists, nurses, and physical therapists, was this note, marked "Important":

Important:
Asking your loved ones about their fears or worries does not necessarily cause anxiety. The opposite is often true. Giving each other room to openly discuss fears usually provides everyone with a sense of relief.

One of the most common and destructive sources of anxiety is the fear of abandonment at the end of life. For many people, this fear can be difficult to understand. You might think, this person knows you love them. You may have not said or done anything that would make them think that has changed, or that you would abandon them—so why would they need this reassurance?

Carol had been raised by a single father. When Carol was fourteen years old, her dad said she knew everything he could teach her. Then, he left Carol in their rental house and moved out of state.

Carol found her way to a relative. She only heard from her dad occasionally.

When Carol was diagnosed with cancer, she was still emotionally close with the relatives she lived with as a young girl. She had a small group of friends from work, some from her softball team, and a few from her apartment complex. None she considered especially close or whom she expected would step forward for support. She was surprised to discover she was wrong. Her circle of support was larger than she imagined. But she did not expect it to last. It was not built on long-term relationships. As the disease progressed and her frailty grew more obvious, she had fewer visitors. The visits became increasingly awkward and shorter. That familiar feeling returned—abandonment—again.

A few friends continued to visit. Carol moved back with her relatives when the treatments took too much energy to care for herself. One evening, her aunt came to her room and found her crying. This was the first time Carol confided in anyone, and all her fears came pouring out. She explained how afraid she was to die, she did not want to be alone in her final moments, but she felt she would be alone. In this heartfelt conversation, her aunt reassured Carol that her family would be right beside her, all the way.

The family she grew up with stayed with her, supported her, and loved her to the end.

When the news arrives that a loved one is dying, complex emotions arise. Preparing tools and techniques to manage emotions can protect you from feeling overwhelmed, so you can stay present with your loved one. In addition to the work you can do on your own to care for your emotional wellbeing, you can find additional support in others, such as professional mental health care workers and people who are facing the same challenges at this stage of saying goodbye. How do you connect with these people?

CHAPTER 19

SUPPORT GROUPS AND PROFESSIONAL MENTAL HEALTH CARE

B oth professional mental health care and peer support groups can play important roles in your work to maintain your emotional health. Connecting with people who share similar experiences, or with professionals trained to assist people in end-of-life matters, helps you feel less alone as you face one of life's most challenging stages.

As a reminder, this chapter is in no way to be represented, interpreted, or intended as emotional or mental health counseling. There can be tremendous value in talking to professionals who help people through these experiences. Professional counselors recognize that everyone's anxieties and fears are unique, and their experience may provide comfort. It is important to find a counselor or licensed clinical social worker (LCSW) who understands their patient's unique needs. In some instances, the patient and family establish a rapport with their counselor immediately. For others, it comes gradually. Some will try one counselor out, then find a better match. Only your loved one will know if they would be comfortable having difficult conversations with this person.

The manager of an oncology care management department, also an oncology LCSW, told me about a family who had been in the oncology care

program through several rounds of remission and recurrence of their loved one's cancer. They had developed strong ties to their support team—the social worker, nurse navigator, clinicians, chaplin, and nutritionist. When the patient, family, and doctor discussed discontinuing any treatments, the family decided they did not want to start over with a new support team. At this stage of illness, patients are offered hospice care, which has its own support team. They wanted the people who had been with them through the hardest days to guide them down this final path. Though not in the routine "right time" care plan, the social worker made it happen. The patient and family got the support they wanted from the team with whom they had built a trusting relationship.

Support does not have to come from someone with a degree or organization to be valuable. However, it can be easier to have difficult discussions with someone who is not part of the family or friend group. Many people naturally want to protect their family and friends, so talking with an "outsider" can help alleviate stress. It also relieves the potential fear of being judged by their closest friends and family. It can help to talk to someone comfortable with discussing death, perhaps their spiritual leader or a death doula. Online and in-person, you may find support groups for patients with life-limiting illnesses. Often people participate in support groups anonymously. A **support group** is a community where people with something very important in common connect, support each other, learn from each other how to manage their unique challenges, and benefit from the freedom to say what's on their mind.

What about people who have not had abandonment experiences, or those who have a strong support group? These fears can still lie quietly in the background, while their friends and family might never suspect it. What can you do to keep that fear of abandonment from sneaking in?

Most importantly, know who you are and what you can handle—emotionally and physically.

If you intend to be there for them, tell them. Do not assume they know it. If you feel the time may come when you won't be able to be there anymore, just be there as long as you can. Be honest with your loved one. It is important not to make promises you cannot keep. If the time comes when you simply cannot see them so close to dying, go to them one last time to say goodbye. You both deserve closure.

Just as the dying process deeply affects your loved one, their family, and yourself, there is an impact on their caregivers. All the physical and emotional support caregivers provide will take its toll. It is important to understand that caregivers need and deserve support. So how do you support them?

Chapter 20

Caring for the Caregivers

There are only four kinds of people in the world: Those who have been caregivers. Those who are currently caregivers. Those who will be caregivers, and those who will need a caregiver.

—Rosalyn Carter

If you are a caregiver, this section is for you. Recognizing your own needs for support is just as important as understanding how to care for your loved one.

The number of caregivers is growing rapidly with the aging baby boomer generation. In 2020, there were fifty-three million caregivers. Forty-eight million of those receiving care were adults with health or disability issues. One in five caregivers were unpaid, and sixty-one percent were working additional jobs. Approximately eleven million Americans are members of the sandwich generation, which means they are simultaneously caring for an adult family member and raising children at home.[4] The challenges of caregiving today differ from even a few years ago, and this will continue to change. Knowing the basic survival skills and resources is key. Each caregiver faces unique challenges—even within the same family. There is no one "plan" that is going to make this experience easy.

Everyone faces conflicts that collide with their role as a caregiver. The person caring for someone close to them, who feels fulfilled giving love and support, will have a different experience from the person caring for someone hurtful and unkind. A young, healthy caregiver may have the stamina to handle stress and physical demands, but they may also be raising a family and working. An elderly spouse may have time and patience, but they may be managing health issues of their own. Though each circumstance has its own challenges, there are common issues all caregivers face. Thankfully, there are solutions, or at least ways to curtail them

Many caregivers set aside their needs to focus on their loved one. Rationales can be "They need all of my attention right now," "I don't have time," "There is no one else to do this," "I'm the only one they'll let help," "I'm the only one who knows how," "It's my responsibility," or "I don't have the energy to take care of myself too." These mindsets indicate that the caregiver has not prioritized self-care. This can have serious short-term and long-term consequences for themselves as well as their loved one.

If you are the caregiver for your loved one, you might recognize some of these issues. If you are experiencing these, they may be depleting your ability to handle the challenges of caregiving as well as your own wellbeing.

- Unreasonable demands from your loved one or other family members—who usually are not contributing to caregiving duties

- Unrealistic expectations by you, your loved one, or others about the care you are providing

- An overwhelming workload

- Lack of control over your time, finances, and new skills required

- Verbal or emotional abuse

- Lack of support system inside or outside the family

- Lack of privacy with no time to be alone

While managing these challenges, the responsibilities of a caregiver can include bathing, toileting, dressing, changing linens, monitoring medications, dressing wounds, prepping meals, and trying to help their loved one eat, exercise, and more. They may handle doctor appointments, finances, and household responsibilities like groceries, dishes, and garbage.

If you are the caregiver for your loved one, the longer you go without self-care, the more the effects are likely to build. Your can-do attitude may be accompanied by the realization that you are having a hard time sleeping or are sleeping more than usual. Your appetite may change; you may feel nauseated or light-headed. You may have headaches or other pains. You may feel exhausted. You may forget things or be unable to concentrate. These symptoms may fluctuate with the changing demands of caregiving. It is important to recognize if any of these symptoms have worsened.

Without making self-care a priority, this could escalate to "caregiver burnout," which can leave you unable to care for your loved one.[6]

In Hospice Foundation of America's booklet "A Caregiver's Guide to the Dying Process," they list these signs of caregiver burnout:[7]

- A strong urge to run and hide from responsibility

- Feeling scattered and frantic

- Major changes in your sleeping or eating patterns

- Forgetting important details or inability to concentrate

- Increased use of alcohol, drugs, or tobacco

- Significant weight loss, sleeping less than three hours a night, or inability to read more than a few sentences without losing concentration

Not every caregiver experiences these signs of burnout. If any sound familiar, practicing these "Survival Skills" can help:

Inadequate Sleep: Not getting enough sleep over time can lead to serious health issues such as diabetes, heart disease, and a weakened immune system. It is also associated with depression, anxiety, cognitive decline, impaired decision making, and memory problems. These can all affect caregiving abilities and your quality of life.

Survival Skill: If your loved one is sleeping through the night on a regular sleep cycle, prioritize your rest during this time. Do not use this time to catch up on other duties. If they are sleeping intermittently and calling on you during the night, ask family to stay over a couple of nights a week and take the night calls. If your loved one is not in hospice, check Medicare for funds for caregiving. Some families use caregiver funds to pay for private respite care. **Respite care** is a period of time when a patient receives care from others, so that their primary caregiver may take a break. You can find options through the National Respite Locator and the ARCH National Respite Network and Resource Center, which provide information about how to locate, choose, and pay for respite care services.

If your loved one is in hospice, request a volunteer from hospice to stay overnight. You may also bring your loved one to an inpatient hospice facility for respite care. Covered by the Medicare Hospice Benefit, this benefit provides five-day respite breaks for the caregiver. Talk to your hospice team social worker to set this up.

Poor Diet: Not eating adequately affects overall health and energy levels. It can increase the risk of chronic diseases like diabetes, hypertension, and cardiovascular issues. Poor diets usually contain a lot of processed foods and sugars. These can contribute to weight gain and obesity.

Survival Skill: Your loved one's nutritional needs now may be very different from yours.

The size, content, and schedule of meals will change with their body's changing needs. Resist the tendency to mirror your loved one's schedule and eating patterns. Though there will be interrupted or late meals, be intentional about eating nutritious meals on a regular schedule. If you are unable to eat well, nutritional supplements may help. Consider it preventative medicine. Eating well for yourself may feel self-indulgent, or nearly impossible with all your responsibilities. Nonetheless, this is a prescription for your health.

Lack of Exercise: This leads to decline in cardiovascular health, muscle strength, and flexibility. It can affect the quality of sleep, increase fatigue, and decrease energy. Exercise reduces stress, anxiety, and depression. Caregivers who do not engage in regular physical activity may experience more of these issues.

Survival Skill: Find an opportunity every day to move your body. No, changing the linens does not count. Take a walk around the block, mall, or yard. If you cannot leave your loved one, find an exercise class on video, like yoga. Maybe a family member could come over long enough for you to go to the gym. Be creative and consistent.

Isolation: This may have the largest impact on the quality of life for caregivers. It is much like the feeling of loneliness that people with a life-limiting illness experience. When caregiving duties become continuous, caregivers decline invitations more often. Social interactions dwindle. Reaching out to others becomes more rare. When you reach out to your network of friends and family for support, not everyone will respond. As painful and unfair as this feels, it happens often. Fighting their perspective will only take your energy. Isolation can lead to mental health issues, poor health habits, increased risk of chronic disease, cognitive decline, hospitalization, and premature death. The problem lies in accepting this as "just part of the deal," dismissing these emotions as uncomfortable but not dangerous.

Survival Skill: Make the phone call. Extend the invitation. Do what it takes to stay connected to friends and family—put it on your schedule. Have a list of people you can call when you need a minute to vent without judgment. Know your community resources. Look into caregiver support groups. When you find the right group for you, you will discover a safe place to share frustrations, worries, and anger. You will find people who share your experience. Some even have solutions to your dilemmas. When you can provide suggestions for them, you will be rewarded with the feeling of fulfillment and appreciation for lessons hard learned.

Mental Health Risks: Stress from this role can lead to depression, anxiety disorders, insomnia, feelings of inadequacy, low self-esteem, social withdrawal, anger, and being overwhelmed.

Survival Skill: Observe, evaluate, and get support. There are several factors that put caregivers' mental health at risk. Being aware of them is the first line of defense. Focusing on your loved one can cause your own mental wellbeing to take a backseat—-way back. Without intentionally checking in with yourself and assessing your mental health, you may miss the signs of a brewing problem. Changes in mental health are usually gradual. Sometimes these changes are more obvious to people around the caregiver than they are to the caregiver themselves. Friends or family who notice changes are more likely to discuss these changes with each other than with the caregiver, delaying support and healing. In America, society is getting much better about addressing mental health, but there is still a stigma attached to it. The issue could also be self-stigma, where the caregiver has negative beliefs about mental health discussions and believes they should be able to handle everything on their own. Part of this is fear of judgment. As difficult as this experience can become, it does not have to have a negative effect on your physical or mental health. Seek and accept support. Take a real break! Not just a fifteen minute walk around the block. Be kind to yourself.

Supporting a Caregiver

When a person takes on the role of caregiver, they will have less time and energy for their own responsibilities. Many issues caregivers face look a lot like the ones people with life-limiting illnesses face. Yet the focus often remains on the person being cared for, with few people noticing the needs of the caregiver.

In both of the caregiving support groups I am part of, one of the most heartbreaking issues the members describe is isolation. They have the feeling that nobody realizes what their life is like, day after day. They describe exhaustion, lack of companionship, and a sense that other family members have abandoned their loved one, leaving them to handle their loved one's emotional devastation. Thankfully, you can help. As with your loved one, there are many ways to support a caregiver, including errands, shopping, pet care, meal prep, house chores, and more. Revisit chapter 6 for the section "Hands-On Practical Help" for ideas.

Try out these additional ways to help:

Ask Them What They Need: Acknowledging that you care and want to help them can bring immense relief. Maybe they just need someone to talk to, with no judgment. Ask what specific chores at home you can manage for them. If they just need a break, offer to stay with their loved one while they get out of the house for a while.

Raise Money: One in five caregivers experience financial strain as a result of taking on the role of caregiver. They may have quit their job or reduced their hours at work. They may be responsible for some of their loved one's health care costs. If they are not on hospice, most insurance companies do not pay for respite care.[8] It is usually paid out of pocket and can be expensive. Having extra funds for everyday needs or specific expenses can be a tremendous support to the caregiver. GoFundMe is a popular website with tools to help people raise money for emergencies, medical costs, and other situations with people in need.

Help Them Find Support Groups: Support groups connect people facing similar challenges together, so they can share stories and advice, boost morale, and find reassurance they are not alone. Support groups exist online as well as in person.

Marsh Mercer's AARP article "How to Find the Right Caregiver Support Group for You" gives information on the benefits of support groups, what to expect, and how to join a group, whether in person or online.

Visit caringbridge.org for information about caregiver support groups with tips on how to choose the right group, including both online and in-person options.

As the Northern Regional Coordinator for Alaska Airlines' Critical Incident Response Program, I had conducted many debriefings and was comfortable with the process. At this point in my career, I had only responded to events that affected small stations or groups. In debriefings, my role sometimes changed fairly quickly from administrator to facilitator of a support group. I thought I had a pretty good sense of how participating in these groups helped people. Until one day in January of 2000.

At 4:21 pm PST, on January 31st, 2000, Alaska Airlines Flight 261 experienced a mechanical failure and crashed off the coast of southern California, killing all eighty-eight people onboard.

Within two hours, I was dispatched to Los Angeles, where I was paired with another CARE team member and assigned to a family of one of the passengers. CARE is an acronym for Compassionate Assistance Relief Effort. CARE is the group within the company trained to support families in emergency situations. We were responsible for meeting our assigned family at the hotel, settling them in, acting as their liaisons to the airline, and tending to their needs for the duration of their stay.

It was a twenty-four-hour-a-day job, where we were available at all times. Families arrived over the course of several days. With each new group came renewed emotions. Many people had died. We did the best we could to comfort their loved ones. Families would tell their CARE team members what they needed, and we would provide it. Sometimes this meant listening to stories of the people they lost. People shared their deep grief and anger. To many, we CARE team members represented the terrible event that took their loved ones away. We did our best to be present with their range of emotions. At the same time, my company was a family. Some of our employees were on the flight. We too lost some of our own. This was going to change every one of us, and my company knew it.

Knowing how important it was to care for the CARE team members, the company issued self-care mandates. The company designated a supply area for the CARE team, where they provided a stock of every possible toiletry, over-the-counter medicine, stationary supply, and more for our care. We received a list of contacts to call if we needed anything not already provided.

Part of the self-care mandate was to call home every night to "stay grounded" and connected to our life beyond this event. Massage chairs were available in the debriefing room along with water and food trays gifted from other airlines. There was a quiet room with a chaplain and counselor. Each evening, we attended a group debriefing. In these debriefings, I learned the value of support groups.

Debriefings often began with asking about the best and worst parts of our day. Just like the groups I led for other events, conversation started slowly. But soon, people opened up. We were amazed how similar our experiences and feelings were. We could relate to each other. It was a relief. We began to accept our emotions and give ourselves permission to feel them. We heard how others responded to similar situations. In these debriefings, friendships were forged that live on today.

Before returning home, we were required to do a one-on-one debrief—sort of a wellness check. Apparently, I passed.

The company's support for us continued. Shortly after I arrived home, I received a company letter that thanked the CARE team and our families. This letter included "special care" instructions. It explained this experience may cause some delayed stress effects. Along with a list of emotional and behavioral changes to watch for, it included resources to help if this experience continued to affect our wellbeing. They offered counseling services with no reporting relationship to the company. The letter also emphasized the importance of good rest, nutrition, exercise, and support.

I felt my company did an excellent job caring for its employees as well as the families impacted by this tragedy. The most helpful part of their support was creating an environment where we could share our experiences and feelings with those who truly understood.

Practice self-care for your physical, mental, emotional, and spiritual health. If you step up as a caregiver, but you do not practice self-care, you will not have the resources to accomplish your mission. It is imperative that you develop a self-care routine and stick to it. Link your caregiving routine to your self-care routine. If certain self-care methods have worked for you before, reintroduce them to your life.

Visit the Resources section to find the "Caregivers Self-Evaluation Checklist." Use this checklist routinely to keep track of your mental and physical health as you provide care.[5]

Connect with an accountability buddy using a similar checklist. Develop a practice to calm your mind and keep your body healthy, like meditation, yoga, or other exercise. Find a support group for caregivers. While your loved one naps or has visitors, check in with this group. Make time for yourself, and you will find more energy to face the heavy emotional lifting ahead. Seek guidance from people who know this road best. But who knows this road best? And—just what is a death doula?

PART 9

OPTIONS FOR
END-OF-LIFE CARE

CHAPTER 21

CREATING COMFORT AND CARE: ESSENTIAL PRACTICES FOR HOME SETTINGS

To help your loved one through their dying process, learning how to meet their needs at home is an important step. Just as essential, understanding your loved one's emotions surrounding their care can help create a safe, peaceful setting for their final days. But if you have not had medical training as a caregiver, how do you know how to care for your loved one?

Until the mid-twentieth century, people in the United States mostly died at home. They were cared for at home by family, friends, or "the village" with little medical or governmental support. After World War II, an increase in hospital construction and advances in medical technology led to hospitals becoming the primary places for end-of-life care by the 1950s. However, within a few decades, the desire reemerged for home-based end-of-life care. This gained popularity after the establishment of the first hospice in the United States in 1974.[1] Home care recognized the importance of personalized, compassionate care at the end of life.

If your loved one has been recently released from a hospital, the discharge plan will include training on what areas of support your loved one needs. If they qualify for hospice care (more on that program to follow), hospice caregivers will evaluate your loved one and create a care plan based on their medical needs and ability to perform Activities of Daily Life (ADLs). ADLs include bathing, dressing, eating, toileting, continence, and transferring—the ability to move from bed to chair. The discharge nurse or hospice can instruct you on best practices, but they will not be there to do these activities for you.

There is no defining moment that says, "Today is the day we make our home safe and accommodating for our loved one and their caregivers." The desire to care for our loved one does not automatically give us the skills or knowledge we need. This section explores ideas to consider, for our loved ones and ourselves, as we age. Some people are reluctant to accept these accommodations. Understanding they are part of life's natural course can help.

Jerry, my daughter-in-law's father, was looking forward to their family vacation in Hawaii, but the rest of us had concerns. Jerry is an elderly man with several health issues—most of them life-threatening. One of his conditions causes him to be unable to walk more than twenty feet without stopping. Jerry has always been self-reliant and stubborn. They had to learn how to accommodate his needs while respecting his dignity. He rejected the idea of any mobility assistance, such as a walker, wheelchair, or scooter. Their journey through the three huge airports was exhausting—and enlightening.

It became clear Jerry would not be not able to participate in some of the excursions planned. But this was a memory-maker trip. Were memories of this trip going to be sad—remembering what Jerry could not do? Or were they going to be happy—sharing as many experiences as they could?

Though Jerry is fifteen years older than my husband Greg, it was within reason that Greg might also need some type of mobility aid at some point soon. Subtly, our son steered the discussion around how useful it would be to try an electric scooter before buying one for Greg. He asked Jerry if he might try one out for Greg and give him his opinion. Happy to help, Jerry agreed and rented a scooter in Hawaii. The whole family had a great trip, and Jerry bought himself a scooter when he got home.

Changes in surroundings, accommodations, and levels of care can be difficult for anyone. Although these new circumstances keep your loved one safe, comfortable, and offer a better quality of life, they are constant reminders of how their life is changing and what is coming. Usually, it is not necessary to turn their house into a hospital as soon as they return home. That's like posting a sign on the door saying, "We're ready, let's move things along." Instead, ask your loved one what they want. A good question is "Would you be more comfortable if . . .?" Over time, keep an eye on your loved one and step in when the need becomes apparent. Striking a balance between observing and asking for their input helps you both decide when to add more accommodations. Sometimes, certain needs arise that require you to make a choice for your loved one's comfort or safety. In this scenario, it is respectful to explain your reasoning about why a certain accommodation is necessary.

Safety First

Trip-and-fall incidents are very common for elderly and ill individuals because of imbalance, gait issues, muscle weakness, medications, and vision and hearing impairments. Thin skin, brittle bones, and blood clotting disorders can turn a trip over a pair of shoes into a trip to the hospital.

Cluttered or poorly lit surroundings can increase their risk of injury. Remove clutter from walkways and around furniture. Keep areas well lit. Motion sensor lights in hallway outlets are low cost solutions to improve safety.

In the bathroom, combat the dangers of wet surfaces by installing grab bars, non-slip mats, and a shower chair. If your loved one has difficulty getting up from the toilet, install a toilet seat riser. A toilet seat riser provides sturdy handles for your loved one to pull themselves up more easily. It is inexpensive and simple to install yourself. Later, a portable urinal or bedside commode may be helpful.

Location, Location, Location

The bed does not have to be in a bedroom. If your loved one's room is upstairs, if possible, switch with another room on the main floor. This can be a den, dining area, or living room—anywhere that would accommodate a single bed with room to get around it. If available, enclosed areas are most comfortable and convenient for personal care. However, be sure to not isolate your loved one. The idea is to be readily available for care. If there are options, ask their preference. If possible, position the bed for access to your loved one from both sides. If they are in an enclosed room, a baby monitor helps you know if they need anything, without feeling like you need to be in the room continuously.

We knew these were the last few days of my father-in-law's life. When he came home from the hospital, we placed his bed in the living room next to the window. He loved the sun, and he could turn his head to see the greens of the golf course. On the first day, we sat his bed up, so it was easier for him to see all of us. The area accommodated enough family and friends that we didn't feel we needed to be mindful of not allowing others their time with him. This is where we said our goodbyes.

Beds and Bedding

Beds are typically flat and sitting-height from the floor. Constantly repositioning pillows to provide support twenty-four hours a day—for possibly several weeks—is not practical. Articulating, or fully adjustable beds, are available. If your loved one does not have an adjustable bed, consider bringing in a hospital bed.

The ability to raise and lower the bed is very helpful. You can raise the bed for assistance with bathing or changing sheets and lower it for ease in getting out of bed. If prescribed by a doctor, Medicare and some insurance policies will pay for the hospital bed. If your loved one is in hospice, the bed, commode, and other assistive devices are part of the services provided. Does a hospital bed seem too institutional? Having your loved one's familiar pillows, sheets, bedspread, or quilt can make their hospital bed feel personal and comfortable.

Whether you use a hospital bed or their regular bed, making the bed for someone who is bedridden is a bit different. If you are not using a hospital bed, consider using a waterproof mattress protector and waterproof pillow protector. Use two layers of sheets, so you can remove one layer easily and still have a fresh sheet underneath. This avoids changing the entire bed every time it is soiled. You can also place disposable or washable absorbent pads under your loved one's bottom. Dark color bedding is more practical. Medical supply outlets have bed positioning pads with handles, among many caregiving aids. Your loved one will eventually inch up or down in the bed, and you will need to move them and change the linens. If they are immobile, it helps to make up a draw sheet to place under the trunk of their body.

To do this, fold a twin sheet lengthwise in half or thirds. Place it on the bottom sheet, perpendicular to the bed, so the middle of the sheet is under where their bottom would be. Smooth the sheet out and tuck it in tightly, so it will not move around and cause skin irritation. With two people, each person grips each corner of the draw sheet. You can use the draw sheet to move your loved one up or down the bed, or to roll them from side to side. This method allows you to reposition them without injuring them.

Pillows

Have you ever gone into the hospital room of someone very ill and seen a pile of pillows? Here's why. When immobile patients have prolonged pressure on their skin—especially over bony areas—blood flow is restricted. This can lead to pressure wounds, also known as pressure ulcers or bed sores. These can range from mild reddening to open wounds that extend into muscle and bone. To help reduce the risk of bed sores, gently roll your loved one from their back to their side and support their back with a pillow. A few hours later, gently roll them to their other side. Four pillows will provide supportive surfaces.

If they are lying on their side, place one pillow behind their back for support, one under their head, one between their legs to support their hip and prevent rubbing, and one under their top arm, like they are hugging it.

If they are on their back, place one under their head, one under their knees, and one under each arm. Use another pillow or towel to keep their heels off the bed—heels can also become very tender. Regular repositioning also helps prevent fluid buildup in the lungs, reducing the risk of pneumonia.

We have talked about their environment, but how do you provide personal care for your loved one's everyday needs? Keep the basic principles in mind: comfort, dignity, and compassion. With these elements in place, you are always on the right track. If someone is caring for your loved one without those considerations, replace them, if you can.

Wound Care

Most caregivers encounter this at some point, and caring for wounds is not necessarily intuitive. If your loved one has wound dressings, their nurse will explain the importance of keeping them clean and provide direction on how to do this. Remember, their body is breaking down, not repairing itself. Their wounds will likely not heal completely. The goal is to keep them from getting worse and to help them heal as much as possible.

Suggested wound care supplies and disposable gloves are available at drugstores and online. Use disposable gloves to protect yourself and your loved one. If you choose not to use gloves, be sure to wash your hands thoroughly before and after dressing changes. Wounds such as pressure ulcers are not always obvious in the beginning. If you assist your loved one with bathing, or if they mention tenderness in an area they cannot see, do not make assumptions about wound care. Follow medical advice. If their health care provider does not explain—ask! Different wounds require different care, but be prepared to clean and redress wounds daily with the recommended techniques and types of bandaging.

Not everyone will get pressure ulcers or other injuries that require cleaning and dressing, but everyone needs to stay clean. Good hygiene is not only for your loved one's comfort and dignity—it decreases the risk of infection. Remember, their body is not in "fighting mode." You can step in to help them as their warrior.

Bathing

Typically, this is not the favorite time of day for anyone who is bedridden. They get chilled easily, the process can be exhausting for them, and they feel vulnerable as parts of their naked body are exposed. For elderly people, their skin is usually thin and tears easily, and other tender areas may be irritated.

For this reason, bathing must be done gently and quickly. At this time in their illness, you may have home health aides attend this personal care. If you are taking care of your loved one yourself, there are ways to make the experience more pleasant.

If your loved one is unable to enter a shower or walk-in tub, health care professionals encourage daily bed or sponge baths. Soap-and-water bed baths take more time, but there are techniques that make it easier on your loved one. Rinse-free soaps and shampoos are effective, and the personal care industry is using them more often today. Several options are available in drugstores and online. Some use water, some are foam-based, and you can dry them all off without rinsing.

The first time you go through the bathing process, explain what you are doing and generally keep a pleasant conversation going. First, warm the room if there is any kind of chill or draft. You will need several bath towels, two washcloths, a clean set of clothes, a basin of warm water mixed with gentle soap, and a basin of warm rinse water. Warm the water in both basins to between 105-110 degrees Fahrenheit.

To place towels, first roll your loved one gently onto their side and place a towel next to them. Then, roll them onto their other side on top of this towel. Place the second towel next to them. While they lie on their side, wash only one segment of their body at a time, keeping all other areas covered for warmth and discretion. Start with washing their top half. Rinse using the soap-free washcloth in the rinse basin. Dry their arm, chest, and abdomen on one side, keeping everything else covered. Then, continue with the rest of their body by sections. When you roll them onto their side, place a rolled towel at the base of their back to stabilize them while you wash their back. Always put the gentle soap directly into the water and suds the cloth. Do not put any soap directly on the washcloth or their body. Blot their skin gently with the cloth while washing; never rub their skin. Rinse-free soaps have emollients that moisturize. If you are using soap and rising with water, be sure to apply moisturizer. It is comforting, and it prevents dryness and

186

cracking, which reduces the risk of infection. Lotions can chill, so warm the lotion slightly before applying. While I was drying Mom off, I set her lotion in a bowl of warm water to heat it up. Rinse and thoroughly dry between the toes and do not moisturize this area. It is susceptible to fungal infections.

If your loved one is using a **catheter**, it is vital to regularly change and ensure the catheter stays clean to prevent urinary tract infections. Your visiting nurse can provide information on how you can help between their visits.

Oral Hygiene

Good oral hygiene may not seem like a high priority, but it can prevent bacterial infections like pneumonia that can come from bacteria accumulating in the mouth. Use a soft brush, foam brush, or small washcloth to gently clean their teeth, tongue, and mouth. Rinsing with a mouthwash is also helpful.

A consistent routine of personal care reassures your loved one how important their wellbeing is. It is an opportunity to provide gentle and caring human connection. It can be a "just you two" time, when you can have sensitive conversations or listen to a comedy on TV!

Yet it is possible to miss the preciousness of this time. Your loved one may be less than cooperative, and you may feel unappreciated for your efforts. Being present at the end of your loved one's life can be hard. Much of the time it will be physically, mentally, and emotionally exhausting. At some point, the demoralizing realization arrives that you cannot do everything, you cannot be everything to everyone, you do not have all the answers, nor do you know how to do everything. Luckily, you do not have to!

Programs for Additional Support

Depending on your loved one's needs, two programs exist whose sole purpose is to improve a patients' quality of life and support their family: palliative care and hospice care. These programs are designed to help physically, emotionally, socially, and spiritually.

If caring for illness was a theatrical play, palliative care would be the opening act, and hospice would be the closing act. The goal for both is quality of life.

"Right time care" means the right treatment and the right support, at the right time.

Palliative care and hospice care share the same philosophy, but they are different programs.

If your loved one is diagnosed with an illness and life expectancy of more than six months, they have the option of palliative care.

If their prognosis is less than six months, and they choose curative treatments to extend their life expectancy, they have the option to receive palliative care concurrently with treatments.

At any time within these six months, if they decide to discontinue all treatments to cure the disease, they meet the main criteria for hospice care.

An in-depth look at these programs in the following chapters will help you and your loved one decide what is best for them.

CHAPTER 22

PALLIATIVE CARE

P alliative care, also known as supportive care services, or symptom management, was born from the concept of hospice care that originated in London in 1967. Hospice care was founded by Cicely Saunders, who became a patient, social worker, nurse, and doctor. She was knighted by Queen Elizabeth for her efforts to establish the St. Christopher's Hospice. Inspired by reading Elizabeth Kubler-Ross's book *On Death and Dying*, Florence Wald, Dean of Yale School of Nursing, visited Dame Cicely Saunders in London in 1969, where she learned more of the hospice program. In 1974, Florence Wald founded the first hospice program in the United States. Later that same year, Dr. Balfour Mount, a surgical oncologist, coined the term palliative care to distinguish it from hospice care.[2]

Who Does the Palliative Care Team Support?

Patients at any stage of serious illness may request support by a palliative care team for themselves and their family. Palliative care may be provided alongside curative treatment or disease management.

Who Is the Palliative Care Team and How Do You Connect with Them?

The palliative care team can include a doctor and nurses specializing in palliative care, pharmacists, social workers, therapists, chaplains, and counselors. They work alongside the patient's primary caregiver. Palliative care can be provided in hospitals, clinics, assisted living facilities, at home, or via telemedicine. As of this writing, approximately eighty percent of U.S. hospitals with fifty beds or more have a palliative care team. In-home palliative care is not as common as palliative care programs in health care facilities. Some programs providing palliative care may limit their support to specific diagnoses such as cancer or dementia.

To locate a palliative care program near you, check with your primary care doctor, social worker, or nurse navigator at your local hospital. Check resources online, such as the National Hospice and Palliative Care Organization (NHPCO). See the list of resources at the end of this book for additional suggestions.

What Kind of Services Does a Palliative Care Team Provide?

When seeking a palliative care team for your loved one, it is helpful to know what their range of services includes. Read their contract or literature to learn which specific services they offer and ask questions if any part is unclear.

With the possible exception of hospital palliative care, palliative care programs may not be as robust as typical hospice programs.

Though not all organizations provide all services, here is the full scope of services typically included in a palliative care program:

- Pain and other symptom management

- Assisting patients with obtaining medications and learning how to take them

- Helping patients understand their medical condition—if they choose to know—and what to expect as the condition progresses

- Helping patients understand a realistic pace for recovery

- Explaining treatment options to aid in decision-making

- Discussing and documenting care goals with the patient and family

- Emotional support for the patient, family, and caregiver

- Spiritual support for the patient, family, and caregiver

- Helping connect patients, caregivers, and families to community resources like medical supply companies and support groups

- Coordinating care if they have multiple providers

One might assume a primary care doctor, nurse, or assistant would help with these elements of care, but this is not the way modern medical practice is typically structured.

A primary doctor or caregiver can meet many of the needs that come with a difficult diagnosis. Additional support is available, and you can set up this support early in the diagnosis.

Who Pays for the Service of Palliative Care?

With several care providers attending your loved one for possibly several months or more, how is all of that going to be paid for? Most private health insurance plans as well as Medicare Part B, Medicaid, and Tricare cover some types of palliative care. There may be out-of-pocket costs for treatments or medications not covered. The type of coverage varies by insurance plan. Check with your insurance provider to see if they have specific requirements, like in-network care providers, or limitations.

The other option for care is called hospice, a program for people who opt to discontinue all treatments and focus on comfort care as they approach the end of their lives. How do you know when it is time to call on hospice for support?

CHAPTER 23

HOSPICE

Over one hundred flights, back and forth from Alaska to Seattle, every week for over a year.

"Ladies and gentlemen, we have completed our boarding process and will be closing the cabin door in just a moment. Please be sure your—"

"WAIT! Stop—don't close the door. I need to get off. I don't want to do this again." My voice was so loud it startled me. As the words blared in my mind, I realized that *I was the only one who could hear them*. I needed to get out of this mental space. I just wanted to get back to my weekly routine: flying, preparing the firing order of things to accomplish, calling my husband to remind him of this or that, finding topics of conversation with Mom that were not medically related or depressing, and coming up with a new meal she might be able to eat. But I could not get past this feeling of dread. I thought if I could discover why I was feeling this way, and why it was consuming me, I could rationalize whatever it was, and life would go back to normal. That did not happen. Now, I know there were resources available that could have helped me identify and address these issues.

Instead, I chalked it up to a hard week at work, not getting to kiss our son goodbye that morning, and—the biggest delusion of all—"This is just the way this is." "This" being the fact that Mom was dying. I felt inadequate. When Mom felt pain or confusion, or when she could not eat, I felt like there must be things I could do to make her more comfortable. I did not recognize her need to talk about concepts of death and spirituality. I did not know how to have that conversation. I could not answer her questions about what was happening to her body. I felt guilty—torn between wanting to spend every last moment with Mom and feeling neglectful of my own family when I was with her. And now, I felt guilty and disloyal for not wanting to go to Seattle to be with her this time. I felt anxious about how to handle what would come next.

I knew Mom was getting close to needing more medical supervision. We were all determined that Mom would not go into a nursing home. Having power of attorney, clear deed to the house, an excellent credit rating, and a longstanding relationship with the bank, I tried to mortgage the house to fund a private nurse. Not an acceptable reason for a loan. Now what?

Most of the time, Mom was lucid, although weak. She was too unsteady to get to the bathroom across the hall. She definitely could not prepare a meal or care for herself. I was no longer confident in the level of care she was getting at home. I needed another week to find a solution. In the meantime, my half-brother and his wife fixed up a very cheerful room for her. Mom went to stay with them until I could get her back to her house with full-time nursing care.

Only years later, long after the need for clarity and answers had passed, did I understand why I felt this way. This confident, capable person was out of her depth in unfamiliar territory. My strategies for handling difficult circumstances had deserted me. Though I understood I did not need to have all the answers, I needed to know how to find the right resources.

Yet I was so distracted by worry and anticipatory grief, my thinking stopped at the first obstacle: "This is just the way this is." I was wrong. I could have avoided most of my inner turmoil if I had known about the support available to me. There was support for medical, spiritual, and emotional issues. There was support for my role as a caregiver. But I was not aware of these options at the time. Why wasn't I aware of these types of support?

During Mom's radiation treatments or hospital stays, the topic of hospice never came up. I never asked. No one in my family or social circle had ever called on hospice, so I did not know what type of support hospice could have provided me through this difficult time. Overwhelmed, I wasn't thinking clearly. Yet tens of thousands of family caregivers have gone through this. How do they do it?

Throughout your loved one's illness or decline, the goals are comfort and support. You learn how to support their decision to seek—or not seek—treatment. You provide what comfort you can. Hospice is the next step in providing comfort and end-of-life care.

There are many misunderstandings about the hospice program, which explains why the gold standard for end-of-life care is underutilized. Some think it is only for cancer patients. Another common misconception is that hospice is a vigil for the last days of life, either at home, hospital, or hospice facility. Another meaning pertains to the hospice insurance benefit. Being **on hospice** refers to both enrollment in the hospice insurance benefit and receiving care from a hospice team. Hospice care encompasses these aspects and more.

Medicare has identified four levels of hospice care, each tailored to meet different needs. All Medicare-approved agencies must provide all four levels.[3]

1. **Routine Home Care**: The most common level of hospice care. Hospice staff regularly visit the patient to manage symptoms and provide support for them and their family at home or a long-term care facility. The patient's needs determine the frequency, duration, and type of support provided.

2. **Continuous Home Care**: This level of care is for patients who need continuous nursing care during a crisis to manage acute symptoms. A registered nurse usually provides care for at least eight hours a day.

3. **General Inpatient Care**: This is generally provided in a hospital, hospice facility, or nursing home. It is for patients who need intensive symptom management that cannot be provided at home.

4. **Respite Care**: This allows caregivers to rest and recharge while the patient is being cared for at an inpatient facility for up to five days.

The following conditions are required to enroll in hospice:

- The patient must be living with an illness, disease, or condition that will result in death. The type of illness or condition does not affect eligibility.

- Two physicians must certify that if the disease follows its natural course, the patient would most likely die within six months. One physician is the patient's primary care physician or specialist. The other physician is the medical director for the hospice agency the patient has chosen.

- The patient must sign a statement saying they are choosing hospice care and will forgo further curative treatments.

Who Pays for Hospice?

In 1982, President Ronald Regan signed the Medicare Hospice Benefit into law, prompted by a joint resolution from Congress. This highlighted the need for end-of-life care and provided comprehensive hospice care to anyone with medical insurance: Medicare, Medicaid, private insurance, or Tricare. If a patient does not have insurance, most hospice social workers or hospitals can navigate the process to obtain emergency Medicaid, which allows access to hospice. There may be a non-profit hospice in your community that accepts patients without insurance and will provide services as charity.

The Medicare Hospice Benefit covers all hospice services and expenses for comfort care relating to terminal illness, including hospital stays and deductibles.[4] There should be little to no out-of-pocket expense. There may be a small co-pay—five dollars, as of this writing—for a prescription. It is important to note, your loved one's original insurance policy would still need to cover any medications not related to their terminal illness. For example, if a diabetic is dying from an unrelated illness, their original insurance policy would need to cover their insulin. More information to follow about other situations not covered.

For those on **private insurance hospice**, the specifics vary between different insurance providers and plans. Some might cover hospice care similarly to Medicare, while others might have different copayment structures or additional costs. Check directly with your insurance provider to understand the exact coverage details and any out-of-pocket costs you may be responsible for paying.

Hospice Is about Caring, Not Curing

Enrolling in hospice does not forgo any and all medical care. It is your loved one's choice to change the focus of their care from aggressive curative treatments to quality and comfort for the life they have remaining. This new care philosophy seeks to minimize hospital stays for life-limiting illness, except to control pain or other symptoms that cannot be managed at home.

This means patients can be admitted for medical needs not related to their life-limiting illness. The procedure for getting these hospital visits paid for is very specific. If not followed, your loved one will most likely pay every penny of that bill out of their pocket.

Your loved one has twenty-four hour access to their hospice Registered Nurse, known as the RN. In turn, the RN has twenty-four hour access to the medical director for their team. For medical issues requiring immediate attention, including a hospital visit, call the RN. The RN may ask questions to determine if the situation requires a hospital visit, or if it can be remedied at home. Revisit chapter 6 for more on this. They will assess whether the situation is related to comfort care for your loved one's terminal illness, or not. Here's the crux. **If it is not related to comfort care for their terminal illness, hospice will not cover any of the expenses.**

If a medical event occurs not related to your loved one's terminal illness, what happens?

To restore coverage through their original insurance policy, the RN will revoke the hospice benefit. **The RN must revoke the hospice benefit before your loved one goes to the hospital.** This way, your loved one's original policy will cover the charges according to that policy's plan, with its deductible or copays. When your loved one is ready to return to hospice, two physicians will reevaluate them, so they can re-enroll. Depending on the situation, some agencies will remove hospice equipment and comfort packs while your loved one is not on hospice. When you are choosing your hospice agency, ask about their policy for hospice supplies during revoked hospice for hospital stays and how long re-enrollment takes.

If the RN considers your loved one's hospital visit necessary for comfort care related to their terminal illness, they will make the arrangements. If your loved one is on Medicare, the Medicare Hospice Benefit covers all charges, including the hospital deductible. If they are on private insurance hospice, their policy will determine their coverage.

There is nothing special about six months. It is an arbitrary cut-off period legislators chose to identify who qualifies for hospice care. Predicting someone's life expectancy is difficult and imprecise. There are many factors to consider. Though the doctor may be able to provide an estimate, that's all it is. So, what if your loved one lives longer than six months?

Hospice care is divided into benefit periods: two consecutive, ninety-day periods followed by an unlimited number of sixty-day periods. The time periods start on the first day of hospice care, and they end on the last day of the sixty or ninety-day period. At the beginning of each period, the hospice doctor will recertify that your loved one has a terminal illness, and hospice care will continue.

It is possible that your loved one's condition may temporarily improve while on hospice, and they may go into remission. If their doctor determines they are no longer declining, regulations require them to be disenrolled from the program. Medicare has an appeal process. Some patients change their mind about being in hospice and want to revoke hospice care. Whether patients choose to revoke their hospice enrollment, or their condition no longer qualifies, their previous insurance reinstates automatically. They can re-enroll in hospice at a later time.

In one such case, a patient found out her only granddaughter was having a baby in six months. It was important to her to be there. She had been in hospice for a short time, but she now wanted to resume treatments, hoping they might extend her life long enough to see her great-grandchild born. After conversations with her family and doctors, she revoked hospice care and resumed treatments. Happily, she was able to meet her great-grandson. Yet the treatments grew difficult for her, and she continued to decline. She discontinued the treatments and re-enrolled in hospice care.

Where Can Your Loved One Receive Hospice Care?

Hospice care can be provided anywhere your loved one resides: house, apartment, travel trailer, long-term care facility, or motorhome! It can also be provided at a medical facility, like a hospital, dedicated hospice center, or a residential hospice.

There are two types of residential hospices: inpatient residential hospice and hospice house. Both are in a home-like setting. In fact, many are converted homes, usually with a few bedrooms and a common area to visit. Your hospice agency, hospital discharge planner, or case worker are good resources for locating a residential hospice. There are significant differences between the two types of residences.

Inpatient Residential Hospice Care: This is typically a home owned and operated by a hospice agency. They provide respite care, mentioned earlier in Chapter Seven. They also provide acute, hospital-level care for management of severe pain and other symptoms. Medical professionals are available at all times. Inpatient residential facilities are for short term stays. When a medical condition is back under control, they will discharge the patient home. Except for a small copay, the Medicare Hospice Benefit covers visits to inpatient residential facilities, when the hospice team recommends them. Currently, the copay is five percent of the Medicare-approved cost per day of inpatient care, capped at the inpatient hospital deductible amount for their first year of hospice care. For example, in 2024 the maximum for the year would be $1,632 total out of pocket. Your loved one may be able to stay longer than five days, but any expenses for that extension would be out of pocket. Rates and regulations are always subject to change. Check with Medicare.gov for updates.

Hospice House: This is a home-like setting structured to support patients' comfort and quality of life while they do not require intensive medical care. Patients who move into a hospice house usually stay until the end of their life. You would likely see some of the same services as inpatient hospice, just less intense. A significant difference is, these homes are not part of the health care system. They are licensed through your state's department of social services, and they are not covered by the Medicare Hospice Benefit or any medical insurance. Long-term care insurance could be used here. Some hospice houses offer pricing on a sliding scale based on ability to pay, but it is an out-of-pocket expense. These homes are independently owned and operated. They are not staffed full-time with medical professionals, but they do work with hospice agencies to provide medical care.

For the most part, families who received hospice care only in the last week or so of their loved one's life, wished they had hospice much sooner. Why do so many delay calling on this support?

If their loved one's doctor has not mentioned hospice, the family may not realize it is the right time to enlist this type of support. Some doctors hesitate to bring up this sensitive topic. Some patients feel receiving hospice is a sign of surrender. Some, who think of their life expectancy as an ambiguous future date, now face a specific six months-or-less reality. Sometimes their family is most reluctant for many of the same reasons. Some are comfortable with their care routine, though their needs are changing.

Understanding how hospice provides support can help you and your loved one make the best choices.

When Is It Time to Bring in Hospice?

Just like preparing the advance directive and will long before a crisis, it is very helpful to learn about hospice, its requirements, and services well before it is needed. Fear of the unknown is overcome through knowledge. It is reassuring to know help is available to those reaching the end of life. Having a plan in advance helps everyone involved. In early discussions of care goals, inform the doctor if your loved one would like to know as soon as it is appropriate to call in hospice. If their doctor determines the treatments are not working, and their condition continues to deteriorate, they can discuss comfort care and quality of life. In many cases, hospice care prevents unnecessary suffering. If their health care team has not mentioned hospice, what are the signs that it is time to ask about it?

Take notice of the following signs:

- Persistent pain, nausea, infections, shortness of breath

- Multiple visits to the emergency room or hospital

- Difficulty with Activities of Daily Life (ADLs) like bathing, walking, and eating

- Increased sleeping, confusion, withdrawal, decrease in alertness

- Desire to discontinue aggressive treatments in favor of quality of life

Who Is on Your Hospice Care Team and What Do They Do?

The clinicians, counselors, aids, and volunteers of the hospice team are very similar to those on the palliative care team, but they specialize in end-of-life needs for the patient. They also support the family through a bereavement period. Every hospice agency has its own characteristics, but they share practices and goals.

As an example, the following is a list of Interdisciplinary Group (IDG) members and their responsibilities for a local hospice organization in my area. This organization provides a notebook detailing this information to each of their patients in hospice care:[5]

- **Medical**: The medical team communicates with the patient's primary physician. As part of the medical team, the Hospice Medical Director may see the patient to assess symptoms, prognosis, or recommendations for symptom control.

- **Registered Nurse (RN)**: A hospice registered nurse manages the patient's care and assists the family. They are the primary contact with the physician. The RN will visit regularly to monitor the patient's physical symptoms and teach the patient, caregivers, and family techniques to maximize comfort. In addition, the RN orders medical supplies and equipment as needed. An RN in hospice is available twenty-four hours a day, seven days a week.

- **Clinical Social Worker**: A social worker is available to assist with the emotional impact of a life-threatening illness. They help initiate family conferences, teach techniques for stress management and relaxation, and facilitate the completion of advance directives. Often, they can point you to community resources for support. They help determine whether home or a skilled nursing facility is the best place for your loved one's needs. They can also assist with financial concerns and help make final arrangements.

- **Hospice Aide**: A hospice aid provides personal care for the patient such as bathing, shaving, linen changes, incontinence care, and oral hygiene.

- **Chaplain**: Hospice chaplains assist the spiritual, religious, and emotional needs of patients and their families. Chaplains care for people of all faiths and belief systems. Spiritual care can be accomplished in many ways:

  - Prayer, rituals, readings, and other spiritually oriented activities

  - Life review, reminiscing over memories

  - Legacy work, helping your loved one leave tangible memories to family and friends, such as journals, letters, drawings, and more

- Addressing any spiritual concerns and unfinished business

- Gaining peace and acceptance regarding the present situation

- **Bereavement Coordinator**: A bereavement coordinator offers emotional and grief support from the time of patient admission until thirteen months after the patient's death, as family members adjust to life without their loved one. If additional counseling is needed for family members, assistance with referrals is available.

- **Volunteer Coordinator**: A volunteer coordinator matches patient and family needs with available volunteers. The volunteer may be involved throughout the illness, death, and bereavement services, as requested. Volunteer services may include respite, emotional support, social interaction, life review, oral history projects, reading, writing letters, and more.

- **Additional Services**: Additional services provide access to dietitians, physical therapy, occupational therapy, and speech therapy, according to their needs. Speech therapy can help your loved one if they are experiencing difficulty swallowing. Therapy in hospice is directed toward training caregivers in safety, comfort, and pain relief techniques.

Your loved one's needs determine which of these team members visit and how often.

Working with the family, the team creates a care plan that sets their schedule. As the RN visits, the plan is assessed to ensure it meets your loved one's needs. It helps to keep in mind, all team members are always a phone call away, when your loved one needs them.

How Do You Decide Who to Hire?

I have put hospice care on a pretty high pedestal—for good reason. Occasionally issues arise out of communication breakdowns or missing resources. As with any situation, there is always the outlier. You may run across an agency that is just not up to the standards. Before you start cold searches on the internet, find out if your insurance hospice benefit has any requirements, such as being in their network. This, for example, is a requirement for the Medicare Hospice Benefit. This may narrow the search. The doctor's nurse, hospital social worker, or discharge coordinator will have experience with local agencies and may recommend specific ones. If someone you know has used a local hospice agency, that person is often your best reference.

Here is a list of helpful questions to ask this person:

- Did the agency respond to urgent matters, or their loved one's changing needs, in a timely manner?

- Did they keep their loved one comfortable?

- Did they explain to the family what to expect from this experience?

- Did the agency explain the status of their loved one?

- Did they support and care for the family as well as their loved one?

- Did they provide the same care team each visit?

- Why did your contact choose that agency?

- Would your contact recommend or choose them again?

Looking into hospice agencies early gives you time to make an informed choice in advance. When you have narrowed down the list of potential providers, check their website to see how much information is available. Write a list of questions and interview the agency in person. Obtain a copy of their contract detailing their services that backs their answers in writing.

Here are a few things you will want to know:[6]

- Are they a Medicare-certified agency?
  This ensures they meet federal requirements for patient care.

- What specific services do they provide?
  "We provide comfort and support for the patient and family," does not cut it—this is too vague. You want an agency that commits to specifics, gives examples, and has it in writing.

- What are their policies on pain management and symptom control?

- What is the frequency of visits from nurses, aides, and other team members?

- What is their staff-to-patient ratio for doctors and case managers?
  A lower rate means more personalized care and possibly faster response.

- What percentage of patients receive visits from social work counselors in their last two days of life?
  This cannot always happen, but it should be a high percentage of patients.

- Do you offer inpatient care options?
  Some hospices have inpatient care facilities for respite care. Longer term care would not be part of the Hospice Benefit coverage.

- How quickly can they respond to urgent needs and what are their on-call procedures?

- Do they offer training and emotional support to family caregivers?

- Are there any out-of-pocket costs?

What if the Agency Does Not Meet Your Loved One's Needs?

Identify the problem areas and ask the hospice director to resolve them. You also have the option of changing agencies once every benefit period. In the end, your loved one's comfort and care are the only considerations—no compromises.

Palliative Care vs. Hospice

Palliative Care	Hospice Care
For patients at any age, at any stage of serious illness.	Any patient with a terminal illness in their last six months of life.
May continue to seek curative treatments.	May not seek curative treatments.
Works with the patient's health care team to help manage symptoms and treatment side effects.	Coordinates most care during a patient's last six months of life.
Private or government insurance cover portions of costs.	The Medicare Hospice Benefit covers all expenses, except respite copay and portions of some medications.
Both	
For anyone with a serious illness, both provide pain management, symptom relief, and comfort care.	

Palliative care and hospice care provide your loved one with multiple avenues of support as they pass through the stages of dying. These programs focus primarily on the physical aspects of care. How do you find care for the emotional and spiritual side of the dying process?

CHAPTER 24

WHAT IS A DEATH DOULA AND WHAT DO THEY DO?

A death doula provides non-medical, holistic, emotional, and practical support to individuals and their families before, during, and after the dying process. Much like a birthing doula supports the mother bringing a baby into this life, the death doula supports the individual leaving this life.

The labor and delivery wing was quiet the night I was admitted to give birth to our son. Greg and I did not see anyone except the nurse attending me. As a first-time mom, I felt anxious. I wanted reassurance, encouragement—anything that said this was going to be fine. It was the middle of the night, so we did not want to wake the family. We figured this could go on for hours, and it did. Babies are born and people die on their own schedule, unless there is medical intervention. So, I placed my confidence in an elderly nurse who told me she was filling in for sick calls on this floor and had not worked labor and delivery for over twenty-five years. She was excited! I was not as excited when she sat down next to me to read a "How-To" manual for an external/internal contraction monitor, while she was trying to put it on me. She kept saying, "Wow, you're either having a contraction or a very big baby," and "Hmmm, she doesn't seem to handle pain well." These comments ramped up my anxiety. I had no point of reference for this experience, even with all the classes, literature, and anecdotes. I just wanted someone with me, in whom

I could have confidence. Someone who knew what was happening. When it comes to dying, this person is called a death doula.

Doula services complement hospice nursing and physician care by providing emotional, spiritual, and practical support. Doulas are not part of an assigned team. Private insurance does not cover their services, nor does Medicare. This enables them to provide services beyond Medicare guidelines. Doulas offer time, personalized attention, and continuity at bedside. They can work with your loved one at home, an extended care facility, or hospital. They offer sitting vigil, conversations about death, and guidance on what to expect during the dying process. They can provide assistive comfort measures such as gentle hand and foot massage, guided imagery, and breathing techniques for relaxation. Doulas practice holistic comfort and may offer suggestions on the use of herbs, scents, oils, salves, and lotions. They can help create a personalized environment of comfort, considering what your loved one would like to hear, smell, touch, and see. The doula provides a consistent presence with no intent to fix or direct in any way.[7] This frequently involves periods of silence, broken only by the dying person's thoughts. There may come a time when your loved one does not want conversations, but this does not mean they do not want companionship. With their knowledge and experience of the dying process, doulas comfort families alongside their loved ones.

Doulas can also assist in creating an after-death plan.[8] Some people want to express their wishes, but they find it too difficult to put their loved ones through that discussion. If your loved one is uncomfortable discussing details about how they want their remains handled, they may be able to express these thoughts with the doula. There are not as many options if the person has died in a hospital, and even less if they are an organ donor. When someone dies at home, you have more opportunities to make comforting last moments for them and memories for your family.

A doula may assist with preparations for cultural customs or rituals. After death, the doula can prepare the room to provide a peaceful setting for friends and family who wish to see their loved one.

How Do You Find a Death Doula?

Doulas are an emerging form of end-of-life support and may not be available in many areas. Check with local hospice and non-profit organizations that may have volunteer doulas on their team.

> Visit inelda.org, where the International End-of-Life Doula Association lists their membership of doulas by state.

Death doulas typically undergo specialized training that includes active listening, vigil planning, and grief support. There are no formal licensing or certification requirements, but training and certification enhance credibility and skills. Without a license or certification requirement, it may be more difficult, but no less important, to do your due diligence. Ask about experience, training, references, and fees. Have a conversation about their philosophy on being present and comforting the dying. If you have a particular request such as massages for your loved one, ask what specific services they offer.

The fees for end-of-life doula care vary widely depending on experience, training, location, and services provided. Some doulas do not charge, but they accept donations. Some volunteer as part of a hospice team. Some offer a sliding scale, based on ability to pay. As of this writing, you can expect to pay forty-five to one hundred dollars per hour, or a flat fee ranging from five hundred to five thousand dollars.[9]

For more information on doulas' holistic practices, many books provide in-depth details about how they serve the dying person and their caregivers.

Visit the Resources section for a few book titles I found interesting.

Help is available at the end-of-life to support the dying and the grieving. Palliative care and hospice care provide services wherever you call home, including long-term care facilities and hospitals. These visits are regular but usually brief. They are covered by insurance. Doula services offer spiritual and emotional support. Doulas also assist the caregiver with physical support or respite. They provide assistance immediately after death. Doula services are not covered by any insurance plan at this time.

The modern day United States is mostly a death-denying culture. It may be difficult to imagine how to support someone through this process. It is easy to think, if we do not acknowledge it, see it, or talk about it, then we can avoid our loved ones' mortality just a little longer. We can avoid acknowledging our own mortality. Whether we are in the room or not, many of us find it challenging to face what is happening. Part of the reluctance comes from fear. Knowledge tames fear. Science can tell us what happens as a living body shuts down. Knowing what is happening can provide solace. Understanding how to support our loved ones can relieve anxiety and fear.

PART 10

THE END IN VIEW

CHAPTER 25
THE FIVE SENSES

How do we know the end is approaching? We don't, exactly. Birth and death share many similarities. First, we are unable to predict the length of labor to enter or exit this life. We do not know the time of arrival of birth, nor death. Another commonality is, the person giving birth or dying is doing all the work. As loving bystanders, we are there for support. Though there are recognizable signs for birth and death, everybody's experience is unique.

If your loved one has chosen to forgo life extending measures and to die a natural death, the following provides a general view of what to expect. Keep in mind, the information shared here is not to be taken as definite signs of how close someone is to dying. Think of these insights as markers for a road trip. Some trips are longer, with lots of events along the way. Some are shorter, more of an expressway, with fewer experiences. What both trips have in common is, they are heading to the same destination. The closer they get, the more similar the scenery is.

Within two months to two weeks of death, an individual's body begins its transition to actively dying. It starts to shut certain parts down, including connection to things outside the body.

Caring for someone in the active dying process requires a shift in focus. The activities of medicating, feeding, and moving all change from extending quality of life to sensory care for the end. Like a newborn, a dying person depends on those around them to care for each of their senses. You can help by learning about these changes in advance.

As your loved one progresses through the stages of dying, their senses change. Senses may become more acute, such as the sense of touch or smell—or dulled, such as the sense of taste. When their eyes are closed much of the time, it might seem less important to make their surroundings look pleasant, but moments of sight can bring joy. The sense of hearing is often the last to leave them.

Understanding the changes in your loved one's ability to sense their surroundings can help you adapt your methods of support. Addressing their changing needs will comfort them and help you accept that you did all you could to ease their way.

Touch

We would like to believe our touch would always show love and bring comfort to our loved one, but this is not always the case. Most people become very dehydrated in the dying process, often decreasing blood volume. Not receiving adequate blood flow and oxygen to tissues can cause fragile, painful skin that is sensitive to temperature changes and tears easily. A bedsore that would have taken a week to develop can now form in a few hours.[1]

Warm your hands in heated water before providing any physical care for your loved one. Be mindful that watches, rings, and bracelets can scratch delicate skin. Your touch will be the last your loved one experiences in this life. Would they like a light hand or foot massage, or hand-holding? If you are not sure, ask. If they are comfortable with touch, try a lightly scented oil to gently rub feet, hands, shoulders, and temples. If they are not comfortable with this level of touch, they might accept a kiss on the forehead or stroking their hair.

Smell

Before you use that lightly scented oil for a gentle massage, be sure your loved one is not having bad reactions to scents. Some develop a sensitivity during chemotherapy, some are nauseous because their body is changing, and smells can become aggravating. Our sense of smell is closely connected to our memory. Smells associated with positive memories can recall those feelings.

If they have not shown sensitivity to scents, and they are still communicating, offer a chance to smell the oil on a cotton ball to see if it is pleasant—or not. Certain scents used in aromatherapy, like lavender, or incense can reduce stress. Most sensitivities are to man-made scents. Essential oils sourced in nature may soothe, whereas chemical scents may irritate. You can also offer items that evoke pleasant memories: a piece of clothing from a loved one, a bowl of freshly popped popcorn on the dresser, or pine boughs for Christmas memories. If you are at home, fix an aromatic meal or dessert, like freshly baked apple pie or chocolate chip cookies.

Unpleasant smells can occur in a room where someone is dying, that are not usually present inside homes. To mitigate them, remove soiled linens, bed clothes, flushed surgical drain contents, garbage, used bandages, and dressings from the room as soon as possible.

If any type of scent bothers your loved one, please refer back to chapter 14 for details to help with nausea. You can take similar steps to help relieve their sense of smell.

Taste

Your loved one's sense of taste may have changed or decreased due to medications, treatments, or disease. Earlier in their disease, providing nutrition for energy was still important. As their body winds down, this becomes less necessary. Their appetite will continue to decrease until they cease all intake at the end.

When their body is no longer processing nutrition, and they have a greatly reduced appetite, offer small bites or sips of anything they can tolerate. Be mindful of swallowing issues. If this has not been an issue until now, revisit chapter 14 for details about how to handle a decreased ability to swallow.

Hearing

A close connection exists between hearing and emotional or physical responses. Sound influences the autonomic nervous system, which controls heart rate, breathing, and digestion. The part of the brain that controls emotional processing is very sensitive to sound, which can trigger strong emotional reactions like joy, nostalgia, or fear. Loud or sudden noises can activate the fight-or-flight response, which increases adrenaline and heart rate. Music and other sounds can release endorphins, the body's natural pain killers.[2] As other senses are shutting down, hearing can be comforting to the end.

What type of sounds did your loved one surround their life with? Did they enjoy the sounds of nature—birdsong, bubbling streams, rainfall, ocean waves, or crackling fire? There are digital devices, streaming services, sound machines, and more that can provide whatever sounds your loved one would prefer as a quiet background. Would they rather hear the sounds of family and friends nearby telling stories and recalling memories? Do they have a favorite book, scriptures, or poems they would enjoy hearing? Or, they may prefer quiet much of the time.

Eliminate sounds that might be overwhelming or invasive. They may enjoy the sounds of the outdoors. But if the lawnmower outside their window seems to be irritating, close the window, or ask the gardener if they can mow at a different time. During the active stage of dying, sounds might comfort, irritate, or have no impact. If your loved one cannot communicate, watch for clues. They may become restless, grimace, or frown. They may moan or try to become vocal. They may turn their head away from where the sound is coming from, or tense their muscles. Learning to tune into their needs will help you create a comforting environment.

I was very moved by a practice in place at South Central Peninsula Hospital in Soldotna, Alaska. When someone is near death, they place a white rose in a vase on a table outside their door. This tells the family they respect what they are experiencing, and it tells everyone working on that ward to be especially considerate at this time. This is a simple, proactive way to protect families from additional stress that may come from hearing loud, jovial conversations and laughter outside their door during this solemn time. When their loved one passes, the staff offers the rose to the family with a note of condolence.

Sight

During active dying, a person's eyes are closed much of the time. Preparing their environment for moments when they have their eyes open can provide solace. This is easier to accomplish if they are at home, or in a private room in a hospital or long-term care facility. If they are in a shared room, use the privacy curtain around their bed and work with the care providers to create a soothing environment.

When a person's eyes are closed, and they seem unresponsive part of the time, this does not mean they are not processing. Do they enjoy the warmth of sunlight on their face or prefer dimly lit rooms with candlelight? If they enjoy candlelight, use artificial candles, for safety. Salt lamps emit a calming, warm glow. If they prefer darkness, place a heavy blanket over the window or use blackout curtains.

For when they open their eyes, have beloved items close by: photos of family events, a favorite art project from a grandchild, or flowers from their garden. Remove items that are less pleasing to see, such as clinical items. At this point, there is probably little need for medications and equipment.

Necessary items like comfort packs can be put in a basket. They will not need a wheelchair, commode, walker, or bed table. For easier access and a more comfortable environment, consider removing these items from the room.

Though your loved one may be processing events around them, they will be missing visual cues with their eyes closed. This can cause anxiety, but it may not be obvious. Whether you think they are asleep or not, quietly tell them what is happening. You can say, "We're going to use the sheet and pillow to move you to your other side," or "I'm going to go lay down for a bit, but Greg will be right here until I come back in." A relaxed tone of voice can provide assurance when their eyesight cannot.

As your loved one's senses change, so do other physical aspects during the dying process. What signs can you look for, to understand each stage of their progress toward death, so you can support them?

Chapter 26

What To Expect: A Timeline of End-of-Life Progression

Three common signs indicate progression towards death: eating habits, sleeping habits, and disengaging from people and circumstances around them. Remember, everyone's roadmap is unique. The timelines are general guides to help family and friends prepare and take advantage of the time they have. This information is meant to demystify the process and reduce fear and anxiety.

Accepting death as a natural and inevitable process, not to be shunned or feared, is key to comforting our dying loved ones as well as ourselves.

One to Three Months before Death

Appetite: Their appetite will begin decreasing. This is more difficult on family caregivers than their loved one. Providing food is a way of showing love and gives us something to do that feels useful. As their body is shutting down, it no longer needs nutrients for energy, so it no longer processes food. They may discontinue foods in a certain order—first meats, then fruits and vegetables. They move on to soft foods, then liquids. Offer but do not push. It's not that they are rejecting your offer, their body is rejecting food.

Sleep: They will sleep more often and for longer periods of time. An afternoon nap may progress to a mid-morning nap and afternoon nap, or waking much later in the morning, or going to bed earlier, or falling asleep watching

TV. These rest periods are not to restore energy; they conserve energy for when they are awake.

Withdrawal: They will withdraw from the world around them. This becomes increasingly obvious as they no longer show interest in what they were once passionate about, like sports or politics. Their withdrawal may progress to not socializing with anyone other than those closest to them, like family members.

Days to a Week before Death: Transitioning Begins

Most of these behaviors will take place in varying degrees within days of dying.

Appetite: They have no appetite. They are not eating enough to sustain bodily functions. Offer a teaspoon of something soft, like gelatin, applesauce, or pudding. They may prefer sweet tastes, since the dying process impacts the taste buds for sweets the least. Often, the ability to taste sweetness remains the longest.

Dehydration: They are not consuming enough liquids, so they become dehydrated. Offer liquids, but do not insist. If they can swallow but are too weak to use a straw, use an oral syringe to drip small amounts under their tongue. You can also use a thickening agent and offer by teaspoon.

If your loved one has not made their wishes clear about the use of IV fluids at the end of life, it is helpful to know what is happening at this stage. Their lungs are not processing the air exchange, their blood stream has slowed, and their kidneys are not functioning, so the IV liquids are not being eliminated. Liquids settle in their lungs, and they effectively drown. Being dehydrated can be uncomfortable. Their mouth and lips can become dry. You can swab their mouth with room temperature water using an oral swab or wet sponge. Be careful to not have any excess liquid that might go down their throat. They could choke. Use a light oil or gel on chapped or cracked lips.

Without enough fluid in their bloodstream to dilute it, calcium can build up. Hypercalcemia can cause confusion, muscle weakness, fatigue, heart rhythm irregularities, and even coma. Without intervention, comas from hypercalcemia result in a quiet, peaceful death.

Sleep: They are asleep most of the time, but they can be awakened. Remember to approach and speak to them softly, to gently bring them back to our world.

Disorientation: They show signs of being confused, disoriented, or hallucinating. This can include talking to people who are not there, or who have died. They may mumble, holler, or talk about events that did not happen. They may behave similarly to the description of delirium. They may carry on loving conversations—and the next minute, shout obscenities. The comfort pack from the hospice nurse will have medication to help with this. If you are not comfortable administering medication, call the nurse. They may make an urgent visit or guide you over the phone.

Restlessness: They may pick at their bed linens or move their hands or arms without meaning. They may move around in the bed or try to get out of the bed. Their restlessness may come from anxiety. The nurse will help identify this and assist with medication. Changes in facial expression are normal, but if they show an extended grimace or furrowed brow, they may be uncomfortable. Check bed clothes, underwear, and linens to make sure they are clean and dry.

Congestion: Unproductive coughing or a rattly sound in their lungs and throat are signs of congestion. A humidifier helps moisten the air.

Breathing: They can change from the normal sixteen-to-twenty breaths per minute to forty-to-fifty. Their breath can decrease to six-to-nine breaths per minute. Their steady rhythm of breathing may stop and start, only to return to a consistent rhythm.

Heart Rate: Changes in heart rate occur. Their heart might increase beats per minute from the normal 80 to 150. Or, the beats per minute may decrease to zero and come back up.

Blood Pressure: Their blood pressure often lowers. Blood pressure can lower from the heart's decreased ability to pump blood, decreased blood volume from dehydration or blood loss, and lack of tone and elasticity in vessels, causing blood to pool in extremities. Cold extremities, confusion, and increased sleepiness are signs of decreased blood pressure. Organs begin to fail from lack of blood flow.

Body Temperature: Their body temperature fluctuates between feverish and cold. If they are feverish, use a damp washcloth on their forehead, replace a heavy blanket with a lighter one, or use a fan—but not directly on them. If they seem to be chilled, and you observe them pulling bedding up around them, add a lightweight cover for a few minutes. Temperature fluctuations can change quickly. Heating pads and water bottles can easily burn delicate skin. Never place either directly in contact with their skin.

Perspiration: They show signs of increased perspiration often with clamminess. Heart and circulatory failure decrease blood flow to the skin, causing the skin to feel clammy. A slowing metabolism can affect temperature regulation and perspiration.

Skin Color: Their skin color changes. Their skin may become red and hot with fever, and bluish when they are cold. Because their heart is not circulating blood normally, their hands, feet, and nail beds may appear pale or bluish.

One to Two Days to Hours before Death: Beginning the Active Dying Phase

In the days or hours before death, the previous signs intensify.

Energy Surge: It is common that a dying person shows a surge of energy. Your loved one, previously confused or asleep most of the time, may become alert and lucid. They may want to eat or visit with family. This can happen with varying amounts of vigor, or not at all. If this happens, it is for a brief time.

Mom was steadily declining, but my half-brother Carl and his wife Bell were caring for her well in their home. They would call me with updates while I was in Anchorage. She was sleeping more, talking less, and not interested in trying to eat. Mom had physical ups and downs, and we did not—or did not want—to recognize that she had not come out of her down times in a while. A few days after my last visit, Mom got out of bed, came into the living room, and asked what they were having for dinner. She said it smelled good. They were shocked. She had not been able to walk by herself for a while, nor had she been eating. Carl rushed to fix her plate. Bell offered to help her back to bed and bring dinner to her. She said she would like to eat with them! After dinner, they sat at the table and talked a bit. When Bell went to freshen Mom's room, Mom went to the kitchen and started doing dishes. Again, they were shocked. They tried to talk her into settling down, but they wound up just helping her with dishes—there was her obstinate side! After visiting a few minutes more, Mom said it was time to head back to lie down. She died before she got to her room.

Increased Restlessness: A person shows signs of physical restlessness, as if they cannot relax their body. This occurs due to lack of oxygen in the blood.

Death Rattle: This is a gurgling sound caused by a buildup of saliva in the back of the throat. Natural reflexes, like swallowing, no longer work. Those sensations are no longer part of their world and do not bother them. They are not struggling for breath, but the sound can be troubling for those around them. You can gently elevate and turn their head to the side to help gravity move the saliva out of the way.

Severely Erratic Breathing: "Air hunger" is defined by taking more than twenty breaths per minute with muscles of the neck and chest extended, working to get oxygen. When this happens, opiates are often used to slow breathing and relax the effort. They may experience apnea, pauses of twenty seconds, or up to a minute, between breaths. They may begin **Cheyne-Stokes breathing**, a cycle of slow, deep breaths followed by fast, shallow breathing, then a temporary stoppage of breath.

Decreased Blood Pressure: Blood pressure can decrease to the point where you cannot see or hear any indications on the monitor. Many hospice nurses prefer to not take blood pressure at the end of life. The constriction of the cuff can be uncomfortable, and they can observe other indicators.

Decreased Urine Output: Urine frequency slows until one final evacuation of their bowels and bladder occurs.

Eyes: Their eyes may be half open and glassy. With thirty-seven percent of people at the time of death, all the muscles in the body relax as the body is shutting down. The relaxed muscles controlling the eyelids cause them to remain partially open.[3] If it seems they are irritated by dry eyes, place a damp washcloth on them.

Unresponsiveness: They no longer respond to sound or touch. You may hear them mumble. Though they may no longer respond, if you haven't done so - this is the time to say goodbyes. As with any time you visit your loved one, sit by their bedside instead of standing. Some sit on the bed and gently hug their loved one.

Cyanosis: Circulation to the extremities fails, causing cyanosis, or skin mottling. The veins in the hands, feet, and knees become blotchy or more pronounced in a lace-like pattern. They look blue or purple. Without circulation, their hands and feet are cold to the touch. This may eventually extend to legs, heels, buttocks, and other areas in contact with the bed, where reduced circulation occurs. Your loved one's facial skin tone may become ashen, and the areas around their lips may grow pale.

In the Final Minutes

Irregular Heartbeat: At the end of life, their heart will beat faster, weaker, and flutter. Signs of a pulse will leave their extremities, such as their ankles or wrists, shortly before the arteries closest to their heart, like their carotid.

Final Breaths: The sound and appearance of your loved one's last breaths will be different from minutes before. This could span just a few minutes, or as many as twenty minutes. They may look like they are opening and closing their mouth slightly without breathing. They may do "fish-out-of-water" breathing, when their lips will "puff" out with hardly a breath. There may be a gasping sound to their breathing, known as agonal breathing. Their breathing may be very shallow with just their lower jaw moving slightly. They may have long pauses between breaths, up to a minute, making you think their journey is over—only to hear them take another breath.

Sitting Vigil

As with all other aspects of their journey to the end, predicting exactly when that moment will happen is impossible. The final moments may be few or many. Even at the very end, be considerate of who they are and their choices. If they are a private person, they may not be comfortable with many people at their bedside all at once. Visitors may enter individually to say their goodbyes and take turns sitting vigil. This can give others a chance to get up and move, or get a cup of coffee. Alternatively, your loved one may be most comfortable surrounded by those who love them.

Many of us assume our loved one would want us by their side at the very end. This is not always the case. They have a limited amount of control over the moment they leave this world. A protective spouse or parent may not want their moment of death to be their loved one's last memory of their time together. There are many stories of family members who sat by their loved one for hours and left for just a moment—only to find their loved one died while they were gone. Without understanding this was their loved one's choice, guilt can compound their grief.

Over morning coffee, I was refining my optimistic list of things I thought I could accomplish. It was Friday, and the list included all of that week's unfinished chores, calls, errands, and the cleaning schedule. Yup, this was going to run into the weekend—again. The phone rang. Grateful for the interruption, I answered. My sister-in-law Bell had a stroke. She had been medevacked by helicopter and admitted to the hospital late the night before. Six weeks prior, Bell had been diagnosed with stage four stomach cancer and was declining. I rescheduled some commitments and planned to fly to Seattle on Monday, then drive to Spokane on Tuesday with Andy, my brother. A few hours later, I received another call. Bell was failing. The doctor recommended the family come see her as soon as possible. I left Anchorage that same afternoon.

On Saturday, Andy and I drove to Spokane to see Bell. We were surprised at her alertness and ability to entertain us with her dry sense of humor. She was sitting up and trying some gelatin. Part of me thought someone might have been a bit of an alarmist. We stayed with Bell until the end of visiting hours, and she was getting tired. We told her we would see her in the morning and kissed her goodnight. Her nephew was there visiting. He was also surprised at how well she looked; she was not the same person as the day before. We assumed she was improving from the stroke.

On Sunday morning, we met two of my brother's adult children, who had driven over from Seattle, before going to see Bell together. We talked about our surprise at how well she looked compared to our expectations, and how glad we were to talk with her.

We went to Bell's room expecting to find her in the same condition as before. More surprise, disbelief, and confusion. Because we had not seen Bell on the day of her stroke, we did not realize what we saw yesterday was an end-of-life surge. It is common, but this does not happen for everyone. It is a short event and usually comes close to the end of life. Just like Mom's rally.

On this day, Bell was asleep and very still. Steve, the nurse, arrived and suggested we talk to Bell—she might respond. As he tried to wake her and explain we were there, Bell opened her eyes. We spoke for a while and listened to her quiet, weak voice. She drifted off to sleep most of the day, only to wake and half-open her eyes occasionally. Steve made several checks: listening to her breathing, checking her pulse in different areas, and looking for mottling on her feet, hands, and knees. We did not see a change throughout the day, while we sat around her bed, telling stories. Around six o'clock, we decided to go to dinner. Steve took our numbers and promised to call with any changes. We all kissed Bell goodbye and told her we would return after dinner. In the restaurant across the street, Andy's phone rang at a quarter past seven o'clock. It was Steve. I believe Bell wanted to go alone.

When your loved one dies, you are left with powerful emotions as well as important tasks. By learning what to expect, you can prepare in advance. This helps you stay present with your own emotions in the moment and complete the logistical steps ahead. How do you balance your emotional needs with the need to address the practical matters of a person's death?

PART 11

THE FIRST MINUTES IN A WORLD WITHOUT YOUR LOVED ONE

Chapter 27

A Room Prepared for Grace

Your loved one's last breath is the beginning of a different life for those who knew and loved them. You can acknowledge these first moments with a sign of respect for them and their loved ones, with whatever is most meaningful to you—a moment of silence, lighting a candle, a prayer, or maybe a religious or cultural practice.

When someone dies in the hospital, there are limited opportunities to recognize this moment.

The staff will offer private time and be as considerate as possible. As mentioned earlier, if your loved one is an organ donor, there will be limited time—or sometimes no time—for goodbyes.

If your loved one dies at home, you can help make the memory more comforting. If a hospice nurse is with you, they will make the formal pronouncement. There is no law that says you must immediately call a coroner. Once the funeral home caretakers arrive, they will expect the family to be ready to have their loved one removed. If you are feeling unsure, a few thoughtful gestures can soften the harshness of this initial separation.

It is helpful to think ahead about how to support their friends and family at this moment. When you observe the indications of imminent death, it is time to call the hospice nurse, death doula, or person you have chosen to support you on this day. Choose a support person who is willing and capable of preparing a comforting environment for loved ones to visit. If hospice is involved, the nurse will help take care of this and many other important details. While family and loved ones are saying their last goodbyes, your support person can help prepare any family or cultural traditions. They can create a comforting environment for those saying goodbye, with tissues and water available. The support person will need to be emotionally strong. They are there to give emotional and practical support—not need it.

After your loved one passes, the support person can have family and friends wait outside the room for just a few minutes. They will remove all medical equipment and place it in a closet, under the bed, or in a drawer. From your loved one, they can remove oxygen tubing or other medical devices. If the support person is not a medical professional, I suggest they leave the catheter for professionals to handle. The support person can remove soiled underwear and bedding to avoid an unpleasant smell. Some will wash the body, smooth their hair, and change clothes.

They can raise the height of the bed if it was lowered for visitors to sit with them, smooth the bedspread, and place their hands across their abdomen. If there is a bright overhead light on, they can turn on a bedside lamp instead, if natural light is not available.

When family and friends return to the room, they will be welcomed into a comforting environment, free from the reminders of their loved one's struggles. This might be a time to call people who want to see your loved one before the funeral home. This can be a time for cultural or religious practices, and a time to comfort the living.

Take a breath—the world can wait. There are only a few things that need your attention right now.

It was almost midnight when the phone rang. While Greg was reaching for it, I was trying to surface mentally and thinking *phone calls at midnight never bring good news.* Greg handed me the phone. From the look on his face,

I knew what it meant. My sister-in-law Bell said, "Patty, your mom passed away."

This was not a surprise. She had been declining for weeks. I had my ducks in a row. I had been preparing for this. I knew my order of operations and was starting my timeline in my head. But this heavy fog rolled in, and I could not move through those operations. It was a type of shock. It felt like all my efforts were just out of reach. I have learned this is normal, natural, and it gets better. You will be able to function when you need to take action. Be gentle with yourself; be patient. It will all work out.

I had Greg call my company and explain I would not be in for a week, and that I would keep in touch. I booked my flight. Greg brought my suitcase up, I opened my drawers—and completely forgot how to pack. I just stood there looking at my underwear! Do I need these? How many should I take? Should I take a hair dryer? How heavy of a coat should I take? In the end, Greg looked at my poor packing job, and he added toiletries, bed clothes, and shoes. I had been packing weekly for many months. I could have packed my bag in my sleep. I was worried about this brain fog and stressed about not being there already. There were people I needed to support, and things that needed to happen right away. *And wasn't I the only one who could handle them?* Unfortunately, I realized, this was the way I planned it. I thought once I arrived in Seattle, everything would fall into place. To some degree it did, but the fog would continue to come and go. There are still things that I have no memory of how they were accomplished.

From my experience, here is my advice: have a plan, know your order of operation, get someone competent and not grief-stricken to walk beside you—and be prepared to hand most of your plan over to them for the moment. You can decide and arrange many of the next steps in advance.

CHAPTER 28

FIRST THINGS FIRST

When a person dies, a process of practical steps begins. Planning ahead gives you more space and time to process your emotions in the moment. Despite previous strength and stability, be prepared to need and accept help.

Pronouncement

If your loved one dies at home and has hospice care, call the nurse. They can make the official pronouncement of death as well as take care of several immediate details.

If your loved one is not on hospice, call 911 and tell them this was an expected home death. Ask that they not use sirens. Be sure to have the DNR and POLST forms ready for them, or they are required to perform CPR after an assessment.

Paramedics can usually pronounce death. Some states require they contact a doctor employed by the paramedic company or associated hospital to make the pronouncement over the phone. The body cannot be moved by a funeral home or mortuary until the pronouncement has been made. If you are using a funeral home for final arrangements, check with them to see if they can make the pronouncement.

Practically, you can keep your loved one with you for up to seventy-two hours, if they are kept cool with ice or dry ice.[1] Your hospice nurse or death doula can provide information on this. Though your loved one would not be able to donate vital organs such as heart, lungs, kidneys, or liver when they die at home, they may donate other tissues. Corneas, skin, bone, heart valves, veins, tendons, and ligaments would still be viable. If they decided to donate, they must be transported as soon as possible. If the family, caregiver, and closest loved ones need immediate guidance, emotional, or moral support for their next steps, fire department chaplains are available in most communities. Ask the paramedics or fire department to connect you with a chaplain.

If you are with your loved one in the hospital or long-term care facility, you can let the nurse know if you would like the hospital chaplain to be present during the dying process or after death. Upon their death, call the nurse to confirm and make the pronouncement. Verify how long you may have their room to say goodbye. Typically, you may have the room for up to four hours, but if there is a bed shortage, you may not have that leeway. If they are an organ donor, your loved one will be removed immediately.

Transporting the Body

If your loved one dies at home, when you are ready, call the funeral home. The funeral home could be a mortuary or crematorium. They will place your loved one's body on a gurney with a cover over them. You can tell them if you would prefer your loved one's face covered or not. If your loved one's body will be transported to another state to their final resting place, they must be prepared for transport by a local funeral home. The local funeral home will also secure necessary permits and coordinate with the funeral home in the destination state.

If your loved one dies in the hospital, they will take care of your loved one's body until the funeral home, mortuary, or crematorium picks them up. Talk to the hospital staff to see what type of assistance they offer, such as contacting the funeral home for you.

Care for Dependents, Pets, and Livestock

Throughout your loved one's illness, there may have been someone to help care for children, elderly, disabled dependents, livestock, or pets. After your loved one dies, there is an even greater need for this type of support for the caregiver. The lives of dependents in the home, as well as the family caregiver, will likely be in disarray as everyone adjusts to this new reality. The coming days can be filled with tasks that may be overwhelming, emotionally and mentally, just when the support goes home. This is an opportunity to help with some of those challenges.

Even at ten years old, from the backyard, I knew something serious was happening in my grandparents' house. The officer and chaplain had been with Mom and my grandparents for several minutes before my brother Andy and I were called inside. Mom stood with us, but she did not speak. The chaplain told us Dad had died, and they left. Then, the house slowly started to fill up. We were surrounded by aunts, uncles, cousins, and my grandparents. There was no doubt that we were being well cared for, but Mom's emotions overwhelmed her. The only thing that seemed to comfort Mom was having Andy and me within eyesight every minute. All three of us even slept in the same bed until the day of the funeral.

This was Mom's reaction to this sudden shock—she needed us close. Many offered to take Andy and me to spend the night with them or take us on outings, but that was distressing for Mom. She accepted support when she went to identify our father's body, choose a casket, buy a crypt, order funeral flowers, and write a eulogy. These were all steps in her process of letting go. But her solace came from looking at Andy and me. A tragedy came out of nowhere, and it could happen again, Mom thought. This hypervigilance is normal. When offering help, trust your loved one knows what they need. Offer what you feel is appropriate and take your cues from them.

Informing Family and Friends

Letting people know their loved one has died is an important step. Yet it can feel heavy for the person accepting this responsibility. Remember, you may delegate some of these notifications to friends and family who want to help.

An organized friend can help notify friends and family of your loved one's death, especially if there are several people or groups to inform. They can handle some details in advance, while you spend valuable time with your loved one. Provide a list of groups or circles that your loved one traveled in, such as their church group, classmates, hobby groups, clubs, military buddies, holiday card recipients, or former coworkers. The person helping you with this can find a point person for each of these groups to collect contact information. If your loved one or anyone in their circle is in the military, the Red Cross can assist with notifications.

When you receive the contact information, divide the notification list into categories:

- Those whom you, or the closest family member, would like to contact personally.

- Those whom a helper or family member will contact individually with a visit, call, or handwritten note.

- For others, a letter in a mass email would be appropriate.

- Some use social media to inform larger groups.

When the time comes, you can divide the contact information among close friends and family to notify everyone. The helpers will need to provide information about a funeral service, memorial, or celebration of life. They can clarify whether donations to a charity are preferred over flowers. If you haven't decided all these details yet, you can still have your helpers send out notifications that explain further details will be forthcoming. In my family, when someone dies, we start the family phone tree to contact everyone.

Inform the following people as soon as possible after your loved one dies:[2]

- Hospice, their doctor, and hospital, if arrangements have been made to donate tissues

- Family and others who want to know immediately when their loved one has died, such as the caregiver

- Funeral home

- Personal representative to the estate

- Guardian of any minor children named in the will

- Friends

- Your loved one's employer

- Your employer

- The military unit they were assigned

- The Veterans Association, for honorary burial assistance if they were a veteran

- Their community of faith

- Service providers such as Meals-on-Wheels, volunteer visits, etc.

- Other health care providers

Revisit The File in chapter 12, where you gathered the contact information you need at this stage.

Expect food, flowers, or other gestures of kindness when people hear of your loved one's death. Ask one of your helpers to keep track of what you received from whom, to send thank you notes later.

Chapter 29
Navigating the Early Days

So much goes into saying goodbye and closing the final chapter of someone's life. Understanding the complexity helps you support the person leading the process. You can also prepare better for your own future.

The death of a loved one is a huge event in anyone's life. If you are the person in charge, do what you can, when you can, and accept help. You can delegate many of the steps that must be taken. Some people find comfort in speaking personally to each of their loved one's family and friends. Having one-on-one conversations, receiving consolation, and human interaction can be healing, but surprisingly exhausting. Keep in mind, the personal representative named in the will may be the only person who can fulfill certain responsibilities.

Setting Final Arrangements in Motion

The sequence of events depends on prior decisions. A natural burial on your property or designated natural setting does not require coordination with a funeral home for services. Many websites offer guidance on planning and implementing final arrangements.

This general overview helps you decide what to focus on first:

Traditional Burial: If you are interring the remains, which means burying the body in the ground, or being laid to rest in a vault or mausoleum, the service will usually take place at a funeral home, place of worship, or graveside. To put together a traditional interment here are some general steps:

- Purchase or build a casket, marker, and burial vault or grave liner, if required by the cemetery. A burial vault or grave liner provides structural support to protect the casket.

- Contact the funeral director to set the date and time for the interment, inurnment, funeral, or memorial service. When choosing the schedule, consider religious and cultural practices, the availability of the funeral home or other venue, and the timeline of cemetery preparation. Determine the availability of the pallbearers, the religious leader, and anyone else you want to be part of the service. Factor in the time it will take to notify family and friends as well as travel time for those arriving from out of town.

- Confirm the venue for the reception, if you are planning a reception after the funeral. Receptions provide a less formal space for friends and family to gather and share their memories of their loved one.

- Once you have the schedule set, contact the participants: the florist, musicians, pallbearers, speakers, and religious representatives to tell them the time and place of the service. *If there was an opportunity in the decisions stage earlier (Chapter Thirteen), selections of the specific flowers, music, and participants could have been pre-arranged, then initiated by phone calls delegated to a helper.

- Prepare public notices, death notices, or obituaries to be published in newspapers, online, or funeral programs. There is more information on this in the next chapter.

- Contact professional caterers or friends and family who have volunteered to coordinate, prepare, or serve food at the reception.

- Prepare the funeral program which includes the names of participants, program order, information about the deceased, and more. There is more information on this in the next chapter.

Cremation: In this alternative to a traditional burial, the remains are burned, also known as cremated. You can choose all, some, or none of the components of a traditional funeral. Prepare for the final disposition of the cremains, also commonly known as ashes. Revisit chapter 5, where we discuss options for cremation. This may include selecting a special urn or adding the cremains to the burial plot of another loved one.

Natural or Green Burial: Obtain necessary permits if you plan to inter your loved one in a location other than a cemetery with a designated natural burial sight.[3] Select a natural body covering, such as a biodegradable casket, shroud, or quilt that has significant meaning for them. Initiate any elements of a traditional burial you choose. For some choosing a natural burial, the venue is often a home funeral.

Securing Their Home

This is a good task to delegate to someone who wants to help. If your loved one lived alone and is now leaving their home empty, it is important to secure their home and property. Lock all windows, doors, side entrances, and vehicles. At a later time, change the locks. Have someone pick up the mail until the executor requests an address change. This usually requires a death certificate, so it may take a while. The goal is to make the home look occupied to protect it from possible invasion or burglary. Configure lights on timers. If you have access to their voicemail, do not change the message immediately. Consider securing items such as cash, credit cards, silver, and other valuable items.

Disposing Medications

Dispose of any remaining medications properly.

If your loved one was in hospice, the hospice nurse can assist with disposal.

If you are disposing of the medications yourself, return them to a drug take-back program at a pharmacy, hospital, or law enforcement facility. If you are unable to access these facilities, mix the medication with an unappealing substance like kitty litter or coffee grounds. Place it in a sealed plastic bag and discard it with your trash. The FDA has a "flush list" for certain high-risk drugs that are dangerous if accidentally ingested. However, many water treatment plants cannot filter these drugs out of the water.

> Visit FDA.gov/safe-drug for more information on drug disposal, including handling instruction of specific drugs.

Returning Durable Medical Equipment

If your loved one was in hospice, the hospice nurse will arrange for the removal of the medical equipment hospice provided.

If hospice was not involved, you may have rented medical equipment from a medical supplier. Call the medical equipment supplier to remove it. Removal may take time.

If you purchased medical equipment, consider selling or donating it. If you are interested in donating home care products such as a walker, wheelchair, or bed table, find local organizations that accept medical equipment. Contact local hospices, nursing homes, churches, VA hospitals, or Centers for Independent Living. See if your community has a "lending closet" for medical equipment. Charitable organizations such as the American Red Cross, Easter Seals, and United Way often accept donations.

> **To Wrap It Up:** In the first twenty-four hours after your loved one dies, there are many steps to take. Remember, you do not have to handle this alone. You can designate friends and family to support you and take care of these tasks. Choosing who helps with each step in advance relieves the pressure in the moment, when emotions are strong. Accepting assistance is key. It helps everyone move through the experience together.

The fog will come and go for quite a while, but instead of fighting it, use whatever energy you have to take care of yourself. Take breaks from your to-do list. Exercise, watch a mind-numbing movie, spend time with your closest friend, hug your kids, pet your dog, order in your favorite meal, take deep breaths, and drink plenty of water. Whatever grounds you to your life, experience it.

Part 12

In Memoriam

For the minimalists among us, this section may be superfluous. Notices, obituaries, eulogies, and celebrations are not necessities. Yet they can play an important role—they comfort the living, now and in the future.

While I was setting the arrangements in motion for Mom's funeral, the self-preservation brain fog was thick. Everything was on autopilot. I had my list—not as detailed as it needed to be—and thought I was the only one who could complete the tasks. The net effect was regret, left in the wake of things not done, or not done well. I still do not recall performing these tasks, but I have the remembrance card from the memorial home to confirm that it all happened.

Mom led a full life. She influenced many people. She loved deeply. She was courageous, adventurous, loyal, protective, stubborn, and had a wicked sense of humor. She lived through the Great Depression, war, marriages, divorces, miscarriages, the great Alaska earthquake, and raising two kids alone after the death of her husband. She was many things to many people. And yet, I did not write an obituary to show the significance of this woman's life. I wrote a death notice that stated the place and time of her birth and death, whom she was survived by, and the location and date of the service.

For Mom's service, I did not pre-arrange the speakers. I just assumed people would get up and speak. No one did. The only person who spoke was the officiator—not comforting. There were no special readings or music tributes. There was a remembrance card, but no program. There were no pictures. And none of this occurred to me until later, when I realized what happened—or rather, did not happen.

These "niceties" provide comforting memories and closure. It is beautiful when a family provides a small momento for each mourner to take with them in remembrance. It is moving to hear stories of how a person brought something special to their life. Reading an obituary in the program acknowledges a loved one's presence in this life.

These are the last vestiges of saying goodbye. Do whatever you decide will honor this person and comfort you and their loved ones. What steps do you feel compelled to take now? What do you want to look back on, from this time in your life?

CHAPTER 30
NOTICES AND OBITUARIES

There are many ways to acknowledge the life your loved one lived. For some, this time is an opportunity to highlight accomplishments or contributions to the community. For many, these actions are their ways of saying goodbye.

Public Notices

Though public notices are not legally required, they are recommended. They help protect you and other family members from the jarring experience of receiving phone calls and explaining your loved one has died. This can be a simple notice that gives their name, date of birth, date of death, and any information about a service, memorial, or celebration of life. The purpose is to inform the community of their passing and allow people to pay respects. Post the notice in a timely manner so people may attend the events. Many funeral homes will write and publish a death notice for you—make sure to proofread it, before it is published. These are not the same notices required in settling the estate.

Obituaries

More detailed than death notices, obituaries usually include a person's history, achievements, education, career, family, hobbies, membership in organizations, and significant events in their life, such as how they met their spouse or began their military career. They may also provide information about services. They are often included in the funeral program and posted after services in local publications. A close family member or friend usually writes the obituary. Online memorial services, such as Everloved, offer templates to help with this.

A good obituary truly depicts the person. Often, they are honest, have a touch of humor, and include an element of surprise. They might say, "One of Uncle George's lesser known hobbies was entering cricket cooking competitions." If the family prefers, suggest an "in-lieu of flowers" donation. If the person died from something difficult to talk about, such as suicide or drugs, do not shy away from it. With family approval, treating these topics sensitively can show compassion for the struggles this person and their family endured. If the person is recognized in a particular profession, have an associate write an overview of their contributions to that field for a trade journal. Publishing the notice or obituary in the newspaper often requires a fee.

After announcing the death of a loved one, people often organize events to honor their life. Many people find getting together for services to be a fulfilling way to celebrate a person and the impact they made. How do you decide what services to hold?

CHAPTER 31
SERVICES AND CELEBRATIONS

M any options exist to pay tribute to a beloved person in your life. Which forms of ceremony feel most fulfilling to you and fit your loved one best?

Wakes

Held before the funeral, wakes usually take place at the family's home or a funeral home. They are often somber occasions where mourners gather to view the body, pray, and support the grieving family.

Funerals

Taking place after the wake, a funeral is a formal ceremony to view the body, casket, or vessel and often includes music, speakers, and sometimes a procession to the burial site.

An important element of funerals is the funeral program. Outlining the events of the day, funeral programs inform attendees what to expect from the ceremony. They also can be a memento to take home. They can have several components.

This checklist helps you include general information:[1]

- Cover page with your loved one's picture, name, birth date, death date, and one of their favorite quotes or scriptures

- Welcome written by the officiant or family

- Outline of the service including:

  - Opening remarks or prayers

  - Hymns or songs

  - Readings, scriptures, or poems

  - Eulogies

  - Special musical performances

  - Closing remarks or prayers

- Obituary

- Acknowledgments

- Photos

- Information on the post-service gathering, whether a reception or graveside service

Eulogies

To honor a loved one, a eulogy is a written speech, prepared and delivered by a family member, close friend, or faith leader at a service or gathering. Similar to an obituary, they include details of the person's life. Eulogies include personal anecdotes, reflections, and memories to create a heartfelt tribute. The in-person presentation provides the chance to add emotion and personality.

Having a few speakers at your loved one's service allows people to share different experiences and perspectives. Suggest your speakers keep to about one thousand words or approximately six minutes.[2]

If you are one of the speakers, here are a few ideas:

- Remember this is about bringing out their personality—highlighting events, conversations, and achievements that show who they were.

- Share a story, maybe one not well known to everyone.

- Write down what you want to say—even if you do not use your notes, this is a good way to organize your thoughts and check for anything missing.

- If you are not a close family member, introduce yourself, so the attendees know your relationship to the deceased.

- Funeral or memorial services are typically solemn events, but consider the personality of the person you are honoring. If it is appropriate, add a touch of humor. Keep in mind, Grandma and the family minister may be in attendance.

- If you are not a public speaker by nature, it may feel intimidating to speak to a group of people, some of whom you do not know, during an emotional time. It is okay if the tears fall. You are all there because you care. This is personal, so keep it conversational. If it helps, talk "to" one person.

- To end your eulogy, share a quote or scripture that was meaningful to your loved one. Or, directly address your loved one. To my husband Greg, I would say, "Thank you for being the best part of my life."

Memorials

A memorial can have all of the components of a funeral, but it takes place after the burial or cremation, so the body is not present. For a family choosing a memorial instead of a funeral, it is common to have a very small gathering before the burial or cremation. This sometimes includes a viewing, similar to a wake, followed by the memorial, a larger event.

Memorials frequently take place weeks to months after the final disposition of the deceased. This gives family and friends time to come through the shock and be present. Also, planning a memorial far enough in advance gives more people the chance to attend. Memorials are generally less formal and include a reception of some type.

For your loved one's memorial, consider the following:

- A funeral home is not involved in a memorial. Instead, choose a venue that reflects the person being honored. A place of worship, the family's backyard, a park, beach, private club, or formal banquet hall are all appropriate options.

- Factor in the number of people you expect to attend.

- Is there adequate parking?

- Do you need to provide tables or chairs?

- If you want to have a video presentation, have the event indoors. Confirm with the venue if they have video equipment, like a projector and sound system, or if you will provide it.

- Does the venue allow you to bring in food, or do they require you to use their catering?

- If alcohol is a consideration, confirm if the venue allows it. Many public parks do not.

Because memorials usually take place weeks or months after a person dies, plan on inviting people individually. Revisit chapter 11 for suggestions on contacting people. You may want to use an online invitation service tol help you keep track of RSVPs. Online services can also help you send out thank you notes to attendees.

Online Memorials

Family and friends around the world can honor your loved one in a memorial space that you provide online. Several services are simple to set up and make it easy for viewers to contribute. Many online services offer free and premium plans.

- Visit forevermissed.com for a wide array of templates for specific themes, such as military or children and everything in between. In their free, basic plan, they offer a limited selection of background music. Visitors to the site may leave virtual flowers or lights. Premium is an annual plan featuring unlimited photos, videos, and illustrated stories. With a premium plan, you may add a custom playlist of songs. This plan, like several others, allows you to login with facebook and set the privacy to public or private. They also offer a lifetime plan. Forever Missed is an ad free platform.

- Visit <u>mykeeper.com</u> for a basic free plan or a plus plan that currently costs a one-time fee of ninety-nine dollars. With the plus plan, you can create a free memorial page, add unlimited photos, geotag the final resting place, and share your loved one's story, so others may collaborate and pay tribute. You can also host a live virtual memorial. This service offers a standout feature: scannable QR codes to place on a headstone to provide a direct link to your loved one's tribute page.

- Visit <u>everplans.com</u> for a list of the ten most well-known online memorial website services as of this writing, each giving you different ideas.[3]

Celebrations of Life

Usually on the lighter side of events planned around saying goodbye to your loved one, celebrations of life can be held at any time. They are informal and upbeat, focusing on celebrating a life rather than mourning a death. Sometimes they include a favorite activity of the loved one, like a game of softball. Like the reception at a memorial, this is a time to share stories, pictures, and memories.

With this overview of various types of ceremonies in mind, how do you make an event fit the unique spirit of your loved one?

CHAPTER 32

HONORING UNIQUELY: PERSONALIZING THE TRIBUTE

There are endless ways to personalize any funeral, wake, memorial, or celebration of life. You could decorate with their favorite colors or beloved hobbies, like a sailing or gardening theme. Serve their favorite dishes or snacks to remember meals you and the guests may have enjoyed with them. What makes you think of your loved one?

When I attended the celebration of life for my friend Al, I was amazed at the displays his wife put together. They revealed so much about a man I thought I knew! Al was a retired Air Force Lieutenant Colonel. He reached the rank of Eagle Scout as a youth and continued as an adult Scout Leader for most of his life.

Al's wife placed two eight-foot tables in a "V" formation with an American flag at the apex. A placard said "Al's Uniforms." Hanging behind the scout table, his adult Scout Leader uniform displayed all the ribbons, patches, and medallions that signified his contributions to his troop, district, and council. The table held photo albums, framed pictures, awards, and memorabilia from many activities he led with his scouts over the years. The table was covered, a few layers deep.

Al's Air Force dress uniform, fully decorated, hung neatly behind his military table. This table was also full. One photo showed Al on the day he graduated from the United States Air Force Academy, next to his graduating class picture, followed by a picture taken the day he retired. There were photo albums of lifelong buddies and Al on different deployments. And, of course, his commendations.

His adult children decorated the table of family memorabilia. It included their parents' wedding photo and pictures of their dad with each of them on the day they were born. Photos showed decades of family events: building a cabin together, teaching the kids to ski, learning how to drive. There were pictures of Al at their celebrations: graduations, weddings, new babies. Everyday pictures showed how he was present in their lives—the memories they will cherish, and the times they will miss.

There was an area that displayed organizations Al supported, pictures of him in the musical group he performed with, and his favorite hockey team that he helped financially support.

Placed at random on dining tables throughout the reception room, we saw pictures of Al at events with friends. These photos sparked conversations among us all, sharing those memories.

This was a time to honor Al and our time with him. This event also marked this significant time in our lives as we grieved him. At each place on the dining tables throughout the room, the family gave note cards with a request that each guest recall something of Al that was important to them—a memory, story, or quality of his character. During the meal, the family asked guests to leave the completed cards in a basket at the door. If guests wanted more time to write their card, they could mail them later to an address on the card. Al's family was looking forward to reading the stories, jokes, and sayings that reminded each person of Al.

Al was quite a naturalist. He enjoyed finding new beds of wildflowers. As each guest left, the family gave them a small packet of wildflower seeds to distribute somewhere they might see the blooms and remember Al.

Al's family took the time to think of things that would help this event bring back memories of happy times. May their creativity inspire you to find ways to honor your loved one and the happy times you shared.

Services to honor your loved one can create powerful memories that everyone in attendance shares. This is the stuff life itself is made of—whether painful, joyful, or often both at once. Sharing life's most significant moments is what brings communities together.

Gwen was one of the most effervescent, compassionate, and dedicated people with whom I have ever had the honor to work. She was an adventurer. She, her fiance, and their beloved dog went everywhere and did everything together. He was a pilot for the Federal Aviation Administration, and she was a private pilot. On their days off, they flew supplies out to remote lodges. Their four legged co-pilot frequently went with them, but not on their final trip.

The huge community they were part of was heartbroken to hear they died when their plane crashed on a flight home. They had a double service; both caskets were in front of the altar. The church had standing room only, with many spilling out onto the stairs and lawn. But there was room for one more soul in that sanctuary. After everyone was seated, and the minister stepped up to start the service, a family member came up the center aisle. Gwen's dog was following right behind. He was wearing one of his signature bandanas that Gwen made him to match hers. He walked unguided to the area between the two caskets, layed down, and did not move until the caskets were taken outside.

Here are some ideas to honor your loved one:

- Collect smooth river stones, or purchase stones online, and have guests sign them. You can display the collection of signed stones in a glass jar, place them in the garden, or return them to your loved one's favorite place in nature.

- Create a compilation of photos and video clips. Set it to music that was meaningful to your loved one, to showcase their life.

- Decorate the reception area with your loved one's favorite colors and items that reflect their hobbies or passions.

- Showcase your loved one's talent or interests with pieces of their art, a handmade quilt, their favorite models, or radio controlled planes.

- Serve their favorite foods or drinks.

- Give guests an item to take home in remembrance of your loved one, such as packets of flower seeds or birdseed, a bookmark with their favorite quote, a homemade candle in a mason jar with their favorite scent, or a picture of them. My husband loves the smell of campfire smoke—I would need to get creative to make that happen!

- Organize an annual event in your loved one's honor. For friends and family who share a passion for their favorite hobby—like cooking, hiking, biking, running, or some other activity—create an annual event or join one in which they participated.

Our friend was a master at dutch oven cooking. He was always the person to outdo at the annual community competition. In his honor, a few took up the challenge of starting a small competition among those that knew him. In my opinion, he still holds the title.

Explore the options available to you. As the person in charge of this experience, you can make the celebrations happen when, where, and how you want. You may welcome input from others, but you can make decisions free from expectations and guilt. My guilt was of my own making. When I was facing these life events, I wish I had been able to read this book.

In addition to the heartfelt ceremonies that often accompany the death of a loved one, practical duties remain. Processing the emotional impact of their death together with your community can bolster your strength to handle the tasks ahead.

PART 13

PERSONAL REPRESENTATIVE RESPONSIBILITIES

CHAPTER 33

WHOSE JOB IS THIS, AND HOW DID THEY GET IT ANYWAY?

C losing an estate is not for the faint of heart. Mercifully, the person named as executor in a will can refuse the appointment. What if there is no personal representative to handle this task? And how can that happen?

Personal Representative Responsibilities

As a reminder, the following information is intended as a public service. It is not legal advice, nor is it a definitive list of all important matters following the death of a loved one. The law and specific procedures vary from state to state, and every situation is unique. Seek competent legal counsel in your jurisdiction. The tasks listed here are for personal estates only. They do not include any suggestions for businesses or partnerships.

Personal representative duties are fiduciary responsibilities. They have a legal and ethical obligation to act in the best interests of the estate and its beneficiaries. Personal representatives must manage the estate prudently, pay debts and taxes, and distribute the remaining assets according to the will or state law, if there is no will.

An executor is the person named in a will who handles the legalities of settling the business of your loved one's estate. Frequently, the next of kin is named executor. As the executor, expect the family to call on you for tasks beyond your line of executor duties, such as funeral arrangements. Though executors may choose to handle final arrangements, you can ask someone else to take responsibility for this.

If there is no will, or there is no executor named, or the will is found invalid, or the named appointee declines, the probate court must appoint an administrator.[1] Different names, same responsibilities—both are considered personal representatives. In many cases, the next of kin, other family member, or a close friend will step up, and the court will appoint them administrator.

This responsibility is often managed by someone still grieving the loss of a loved one. Managing these affairs can be an unfamiliar task. Because of this, it is worth considering legal and financial counseling for this process.

Now that you know who is involved in this stage of the process and how these roles are filled, what exactly do they do?

CHAPTER 34

OUTLINE OF DUTIES

O n average, there are over one hundred tasks associated with settling an estate. The list here is a brief overview of these responsibilities. For this reason, I suggest using a free online guide—including detailed checklists—to organize the steps.

Here are two excellent resources that offer interactive experiences:

- Visit executor.org for the article "15 Primary Roles and Duties of an Executor," which sensitively addresses the human side of processing death. For practical matters of settling someone's affairs, their detailed website thoroughly covers the bases.

- Visit joincake.com for the "Post Loss Checklist" that covers all topics relating to end-of-life issues.

Not every task listed below will apply. If there is a surviving family member in the shared home, they can handle some of these tasks. If there is an extensive estate, there may be additional steps. It is common for the process to take a year, including a lot of duplicated effort. This book will not discuss trusts because they can be complicated, and they are unique to each case. Unless you are an estate lawyer, I would suggest you consult one.

Obtain the Death Certificate

In a traditional burial, the funeral home can assist with obtaining the death certificate. Death certificates are also available at your county vital records office. There is no limit to the number you may request, but there is a fee for each. In my community, they are twenty-five dollars for an original certified copy. It is generally recommended you obtain about fifteen original copies. Many of the institutions you will be working with, such as credit card companies, financial institutions, and insurance companies, will not discuss your loved one's account with you without a death certificate.

Why So Many Copies?

These entities currently require **original** copies of the death certificate:[2]

- Life and health insurance—to limit fraud and to ensure the individual is deceased

- 401K and retirement plans

- Military benefits

- Out-of-state bank accounts

- Title transfers

- State tax returns

- Transporting human remains. If your loved one is transferred to another funeral home in another state, that funeral home will take care of permits and documentation. If you are taking their ashes through TSA, keep an original death certificate on hand.

- Stock certificates, bonds, and money market accounts

These organizations currently accept **photocopies** or **scans** of certified copies:[2]

- Credit bureaus will require a written notice of death. They cannot automatically put in the term that someone died, so they want you to request them to add the term "deceased" to their credit report. They also require a copy of the death certificate, which can be mailed or sent digitally.

- Cell phone providers

- In-state banks

- DMV

- Family members' employers might allow bereavement time if their employee provides a death certificate.

File the Will with the Probate Court

The probate court will validate the will by notifying all interested parties about the probate proceedings. They will check for your loved one's signature to verify its authenticity. They will also ensure the required number of witness signatures are present. In addition, they will confirm the statement is present that your loved one was of sound mind and not under duress at the time they signed the will.[3]

The court may hold a hearing if interested parties contest the validity of the will. If the court finds the will valid, it will issue an order that officially recognizes the will. Then, they will appoint the executor or administrator.

Obtain Letters of Administration,□ Representation, or Testamentary

If you are the executor, the probate court will issue you a letter of testamentary. If you are an appointed administrator, the court will issue you a letter of administration or representation. These documents give you the authority to settle the business of the estate.

Gather All Legal and Financial Documents that Apply Solely to the Deceased

Using the list in chapter 5, collect all documents, records, and accounts. Verify the information is current and complete. You will need these documents to handle the tasks necessary to close the estate.

Notify Important Institutions

Plan on communicating with everyone listed in The File. Some are time sensitive—identify these first.

Notify the following:

- **Social Security Administration (SSA)**: Funeral homes will likely notify the Social Security Administration. The SSA will in turn notify Medicare. If you did not use the services of a funeral home, mortuary, or crematorium, it is important to notify the SSA as soon as possible. Currently, you must return SSA benefits for the month in which the person dies. The SSA pays benefits for the previous month. If someone dies in February, the check received in March is payment for February; therefore, you must send back the check received in March and any subsequent payments. Beneficiaries may be entitled to a modest death benefit from the SSA. To prevent identity theft and fraud, the SSA will place your loved one's social security number on the Death Master File (DMF).

- **Accounts**: Financial institutions, credit card companies, utilities, and any other creditors that the deceased had a joint account with, are subject to different methods of resolution depending on the type of joint account and its terms. If you have questions about resolving any of these accounts, consult the company, an accountant, or attorney. In some cases, such as a Joint Account with Rights of Survivorship, the surviving account holder automatically assumes full ownership of the account. They can continue to use the account without interruption, and the account does not go through probate.

- **Post Office**: If you shared a home with the deceased, you may open and manage their mail as needed. Contact each sender and inform them to stop sending mail. If you did not share a home with the deceased, you will need to provide proof that you are their personal representative and complete a Change of Address order with the Post Office.

Notify these additional government agencies and programs of a death:[4]

- **IRS**: File the person's final income tax returns.

- **State Social Services Office**: Cancel payments for benefit programs such as SNAP (food stamps), TANF (welfare), rental assistance, and Medicaid.

- **Veterans Association (VA)**: If your loved one was a veteran, notify the VA in order to receive burial benefits, death benefits, survivor benefits, and veterans life insurance. Be sure to cancel these benefits: compensation, pension, education, and health.

- **Defense Finance and Accounting Service (DFAS):** If your loved one was a military retiree, notify the DFAS to receive military retiree benefits, stop pension payments, and submit forms for the Survivor Benefit Plan, if the person was enrolled.

- **Office of Personnel Management (OPM):** If your loved one was a federal employee or retiree, notify OPM to receive federal employee benefits. They will help process any annuity due to survivors.

- **United States Department of State:** Return their US passport along with a certified copy of the death certificate and letter requesting the cancellation or destruction of the passport. This helps prevent identity theft.

- **Local Election Office:** Cancel the person's voter registration. This helps prevent voter fraud.

Here are the common responsibilities of the personal representative:

- Obtain a copy of the will and file it with the local probate court.

- Obtain copies of the death certificate.

- Notify banks, credit card companies, other creditors, and government agencies of the death.

- Determine what type of probate process is necessary and represent the estate in probate court.

- Establish a bank account for the estate and pay any ongoing bills.

- File an inventory of the estate's assets with the court.

- Maintain the property until it can be distributed or sold.

- If you are a surviving joint owner, have jointly owned property transferred into your name alone.

- Pay the estate's debts and taxes.

- Distribute assets to beneficiaries according to the will.

- Dispose of any remaining property.

CHAPTER 35

VULNERABILITIES

Sage wisdom advises to delay making any major decisions within the first six months to a year. Take your time and get good advice.

People grieving the loss of a loved one can be particularly vulnerable to exploitation in several areas:[5]

Financial Scams: The bereaved are frequently targets for fraudulent schemes such as fake investment opportunities, offers to purchase your home, or phishing scams. Be cautious with unsolicited offers. Verify the identity of anyone requesting financial information and consult with a trusted financial advisor before making any financial decisions.

Identity Theft of the Deceased: Beware this alternative definition of "ghosting!" Identity theft can cause survivors financial loss, legal complications, privacy invasion, emotional stress, and delays to settling the estate. Notify financial institutions, credit bureaus, and government agencies of the death to prevent misuse of the deceased's information. Be cautious about including details about survivors such as birth dates in electronic memorials.

Unethical People: All of a sudden, they can come out of the woodwork. They are more likely to take advantage of recently bereaved families by trying to sell them unnecessary or overpriced products and services such as automobile or home repair. They may try to exploit emotional vulnerability by trying to borrow money or ask for favors. Unscrupulous individuals may attempt to manipulate legal documents or pressure the bereaved into signing agreements not in their best interest. Address these situations by first doing your research: get bids, references, or legal advice, and set boundaries.

Other Good Advice:

- Establish an early relationship with your attorney. Seeking their advice may avoid costly additional legal services later.

- Do not pay off the deceased person's debts from your own funds. The estate is responsible for paying off any debts of the deceased. Paying off their debts only increases the net value of the estate, which may mean you would have to pay higher inheritance taxes.

- Do not ignore creditors. Tell them your loved one is deceased and explain they must wait until an executor is appointed. Do not agree or sign anything without discussing it with your attorney.

- As a beneficiary, avoid immediate collection of benefits. First, determine if there are tax repercussions for accepting or refusing an asset. An attorney can help you find the best approach.

- If you are a surviving spouse, do not remove your spouse immediately from your credit card accounts. It can be a complex process to remove a deceased spouse from a joint account. Closing the joint accounts may affect your credit score. You may need the credit line for essential expenses, especially while the estate is being settled. Consider waiting six months to open an account in your name only.

- Avoid lifestyle changes. Take time to reflect on how the loss will affect your family and friends, and how the new situation or distributions will affect everyone's lives.

- To limit your exposure and prevent unwanted offers from ending up in the wrong hands, consider opting out of prescreened offers and direct marketing.

  - Visit <u>optoutprescreen.com</u>to permanently opt out of pre-screened offers.

  - Visit <u>dmachoice.org</u> to register with the Direct Marketing Association's (DMA) Mail Preference Service (MPS) and prevent unwanted offers via the mail. Registering opts you out of receiving unsolicited mail for five years. This will reduce most unsolicited mail. However, your registration will not stop mailings from organizations that do not use the DMA's Mail Preference Service.

  - Visit <u>donotcall.gov</u> or call 1-888-382-1222 to register on the National Do Not Call Registry and prevent unwanted calls.

I have been involved in settling several estates, and each was different. Some were complicated. Others were simple. All were difficult. Not necessarily because of the responsibilities involved, but because of what this process represents: closing a door that will never open again. Though this is the business side of life, these tasks can keep emotions raw. Be kind to yourself. The end of an estate is not the end of grieving.

PART 14

GRIEF AND BEREAVEMENT

CHAPTER 36
THE MOURNER'S BILL OF RIGHTS

Did you know that mourners have a bill of rights? Written by Dr. Alan Wolfelt, "The Mourner's Bill of Rights" establishes understandings about how people grieve and how to respect their needs and boundaries.

The Mourner's Bill of Rights

Though you should reach out to others as you do the work of mourning, you should not feel obligated to accept the unhelpful responses you may receive from some people. You are the one who is grieving, and as such, you have certain "rights" no one should try to take away from you.

The following list is intended both to empower you to heal and to decide how others can and cannot help. This is not to discourage you from reaching out to others for help, but rather to assist you in distinguishing useful responses from hurtful ones.

1. **You have the right to experience your own unique grief.** No one else will grieve in the exact same way you do. So, when you turn to others for help, don't allow them to tell you what you should or should not be feeling.

2. **You have the right to talk about your grief.** Talking about your grief will help you heal. Seek out others who will allow you to talk as much as you want about your grief. If at times you do not feel like talking, you also have the right to be silent.

3. **You have the right to feel a multitude of emotions.** Confusion, disorientation, fear, guilt, and relief are just a few of the emotions you might feel as part of your grief journey. Others may try to tell you that feeling angry, for example, is wrong. Don't take these judgmental responses to heart. Instead, find listeners who will accept your feelings without conditions.

4. **You have the right to be tolerant of your physical and emotional limits.** Your feelings of loss and sadness will probably leave you feeling fatigued. Respect what your body and mind are telling you. Get daily rest. Eat balanced meals. And don't allow others to push you into doing things you don't feel ready to do.

5. **You have the right to experience "grief bursts."** Sometimes, out of nowhere, a powerful surge of grief may overcome you. This can be frightening, but it is normal and natural. Find someone who understands and will let you talk it out.

6. **You have the right to make use of ritual.** The funeral ritual does more than acknowledge the death of someone loved. It helps provide you with the support of caring people. More importantly, the funeral is a way for you to mourn. If others tell you the funeral or other healing rituals such as these are silly or unnecessary, don't listen.

7. **You have the right to embrace your spirituality.** If faith is a part of your life, express it in ways that seem appropriate to you. Allow yourself to be around people who understand and support your

religious beliefs. If you feel angry at God, find someone to talk with who won't be critical of your feelings of hurt and abandonment.

8. **You have the right to search for meaning.** You may find yourself asking, "Why did he or she die? Why this way? Why now?" Some of your questions may have answers, but some may not. And watch out for the clichéd responses some people may give you. Comments like, "It was God's will" or "Think of what you have to be thankful for" are not helpful and you do not have to accept them.

9. **You have the right to treasure your memories.** Memories are one of the best legacies that exist after the death of someone loved. You will always remember. Instead of ignoring your memories, find others with whom you can share them.

10. **You have the right to move toward your grief and heal.** Reconciling your grief will not happen quickly. Remember, grief is a process, not an event. Be patient and tolerant with yourself and avoid people who are impatient and intolerant with you. Neither you nor those around you must forget that the death of someone loved changes your life forever.

Reprinted with permission from "*The Mourner's Bill of Rights*" by Alan D. Wolfelt, Ph.D. For more information on grief and healing and to order Dr. Wolfelt's books, visit www.centerforloss.com. The Mourner's Bill of Rights Alan D. Wolfelt, Ph.D., C.T., www.centerforloss.com[1]

For those who have not experienced the death of a loved one firsthand, the concept of grief can seem one-dimensional. In reality, grief takes many forms. Anticipatory grief is the feeling of loss that some feel *before* the loss actually occurs. It encompasses a range of emotions, such as sadness, fear, anger, and even guilt. It allows people to prepare emotionally and mentally for the impending loss, with time to seek support and say goodbyes in meaningful ways. Grief is the intense emotional pain and sorrow you feel *after* someone you love dies. It can feel overwhelming and all-consuming. Yet, it is only part of the overall experience.

Bereavement is the period of mourning and adjustment following the loss of a loved one. It can feel profound because it includes the emotional aspects of grief as well as the practical and social adjustments that come with losing someone close. It involves significant changes in your daily life, routines, and relationships, which add to the emotional turmoil.

Most importantly, each person's bereavement is unique and personal. There is no right or wrong way to grieve. There is no timeline.

To help understand the grieving process, did you know a model exists that establishes five stages of grief?

CHAPTER 37

STAGES AND OTHER ASPECTS OF GRIEF

G rief can feel isolating, like you are on your own in uncharted waters. Yet grief is one part of life all people experience. The five stages of grief is a well-known model that has helped many people understand their deeply personal process of mourning and realize they are not alone. In 1969, Dr. Elizabeth Kubler-Ross proposed her model of the five stages of grief in her book *On Death and Dying*.[2] She first presented them sequentially, which was misunderstood as a rigid progression. The stages are useful to understand, but not everyone goes through all stages, nor do they progress in the same order. Some experience multiple stages simultaneously. Some people repeat stages.

The five stages of grief model helps us understand the emotional path many people experience:

- **Denial**: This defense mechanism helps people cope with the shock of their loved one's death. Even those present throughout their loved one's illness, transition, and death may still experience shock.

- **Anger**: Many people feel anger, often directed at their loved one, themselves, other people, or a higher power. A grieving person may feel frustrated, betrayed, or resentful. This can also include guilt—*How can I be mad at you for dying?*

- **Bargaining**: This is an attempt to regain control or avoid the pain of loss. A grieving person may try to make deals or promises with themselves, other people, or a higher power.

- **Depression**: This can set in when a person realizes their loss is final. This often comes with feelings of sadness, hopelessness, emptiness, and loneliness. Some notice changes in their sleeping and eating habits—sometimes sleeping or eating too little, or sleeping or eating too much. They may lose interest in activities or withdraw from others.

- **Acceptance**: This is a stage of peace that comes from acknowledging loss and finding new ways to cope.

The uniqueness of each person's experience makes it impossible to predict every impact their grief may have. The danger in highlighting typical challenges is that someone might experience something different, which could cause anxiety. Fear, physical symptoms, and regret are present during almost everyone's journey through grief. To be able to recognize these responses as normal may prevent additional stress.

Fear is a fundamental element of grief. The death of someone close is a reminder of our own mortality—of how little control we have over our lives. You may fear the future without your loved one, loneliness, change, vulnerability, or judgement. You may fear that your memories of your loved one will fade.[2]

Physical symptoms of grief are as real as the painful emotions you feel. Some experience shortness of breath, tightening in their chest, an irregular heartbeat, or a knot in their stomach. If you are experiencing serious physical symptoms, contact your doctor.

Regret is a common element of grief. It is normal to regret things you did or did not do, things you did or did not say, and missed opportunities.

Realizing that the chance to change is gone forever can add another layer of sadness and a sense of unfinished business. One of the biggest regrets is not saying goodbye. How can you protect yourself from this regret?

CHAPTER 38

WHAT IF YOU DIDN'T SAY GOODBYE?

Saying goodbye provides closure and healing. It is an opportunity to take care of unfinished business. Not having this experience while your loved one was alive can add regret, anxiety, and shame to grief. For any reason, if you did not say goodbye directly to your loved one, you can say goodbye in other ways and find closure.

Grief takes its own route, in its own time, but there are a few ideas that might help ease these feelings:

- Honor your loved one. If they supported a charitable organization, consider volunteering or donating in their honor.

- Visit a place that had special meaning to your loved one, such as a park, fishing hole, or vantage point on a favorite scenic drive. Have this farewell conversation there. Tell them how you feel about not saying goodbye. Say everything you wish you had said. Share a favorite memory of a time you had together or what you will miss most about them. Take as long as you need. Then say goodbye.

- Check in on their family. Call their parents or siblings.

- Visit their grave.

- Write all your thoughts and feelings in a letter. The physical act of writing can be healing. Consider sharing the letter with someone close who knows the pain you are going through. You can burn the letter and spread the ashes at a favorite hiking trail, fishing hole, garden, or under a tree planted in their honor.

CHAPTER 39
REDISCOVERY AND SELF-CARE

R ediscovery is part of the bereavement period. You might only see yourself through your relationship with your loved one. This can be especially true for long relationships. Rediscovery is the process by which you return to yourself, "rediscovering" who you are after these life experiences have shaped you in new ways.

Cathy is an intelligent, independent woman with her own opinions. Married for over forty years, she and Will spent all their time together until his death. She describes him as her best friend. She and her best friend were joined at the hip; they became one. With Will's death, she felt like half of her was gone. She was always interested in his opinions and valued his input into her decisions. But when she turned to his chair to say something, he was not there. Of course she missed him, but this was different. Her partner was gone.

One day, as we were talking about the changes in her life, she told me she needed time to figure out who she was without Will. She realized that she needed new processes. She was learning to be comfortable without having someone to bounce ideas off, or to share a passing thought. She would now make decisions without considering someone else's preference. This adjustment comes to those who lose a life partner, to one degree or another. It is a necessary part of the healing process.

A family caregiver's rediscovery can be somewhat different. They devoted most of their physical, mental, and emotional energy to one purpose: the care of their loved one at the end of their life. It can be exhausting and all consuming—and in the timespan of one breath, it is over. The changes in their priorities and sense of purpose do not adjust so quickly. If the family caregiver is also the executor, their rediscovery will have to wait. Support groups exist for family caregivers specifically after their loved one dies. You can find support groups in person, online, and in facebook groups.

Healing takes time and self-care. You will recognize some of these tips as strategies for caregiver stress relief:[4]

- **Learn about Your Grief**: Knowing how grief affects you is one way of taking care of yourself. When you know what to expect and learn coping techniques, you will worry less.

- **Eat Healthy**: Grief and stress rob your body of energy. Without proper nutrition, you may start to feel dizzy or unable to keep up with your normal activities.

- **Sleep**: Get enough rest. This may be difficult, especially in the first few days. Try meditation, relaxing music, and a warm, non-caffeinated drink. If these do not help, you may want to contact your doctor. Also contact them if you are sleeping too much. This can be a sign of depression.

- **Exercise**: Get enough physical activity. Walk, take an exercise class, or yoga. Try what your doctor recommends.

- **Keep in Touch with Your Support Network**: A coffee date with a trusted friend, a phone call, or video chat to share your loss, will help with stress and lift your spirits. Isolation can lead to depression.

- **Journal**: Journaling brings order to our thoughts and relieves stress. Let your writing flow. Include your thoughts, feelings, and memories of your loved one. Write about events that triggered a burst of grief and how you handled it. Describe something you are looking forward to experiencing. Write about anything you want.

- **Listen to Music**: It can be soothing, energizing, and spiritually uplifting.

- **Do Something for Yourself**: Recharge by taking time away from the world for "you" time. You might enjoy a warm bath and soothing music, or uninterrupted quiet to read in your room.

- **Stop Apologizing**: You do not need to apologize for feeling the heightened emotions and reactions you experience while grieving. Feeling overwhelmed and emotional is normal. These feelings will even out over time. You do not need to feel sorry for saying no.

- **Consider Counseling**: When you feel overwhelmed, or life becomes too difficult during tough times, speak to a professional with experience in grief. You can connect with a counselor online or in person.

Grief and bereavement are difficult to navigate because there is no way to predict or control your progress through these stages. Neither medications nor kind words will heal the pain—only time. It can feel scary and frustrating to discover that tomorrow will not necessarily be better than today. But it will be better someday. In my experience, the deep sorrow will fade, and we will still have who they were with us.

Some believe the price of love is the grief we feel when our loved one is gone. I spoke to my friend Tom today who shared his thoughts on this. Tom will attend his son's funeral this weekend. Through tears, Tom said, "The price of the ticket was worth the ride."

Resources

Part 1: Reluctant Compassion
- caringbridge.org/resources/helping/what-to-say - This article "What to say" provides guidance for those giving, or responding to, the news of serious illness, impending death, or other difficult conversations at the end of life.

Part 2: Everyone Plays a Part
- everplans.com - This website provides worksheets and suggestions on how to compose an ethical will.

- shutterfly.com, mixbook.com, snapfish.com - These services offer tools for you to create photo books of personal history.

Part 5: Decisions to Make, Communicate, and Record
- theconversationproject.org - This program guide facilitates conversations with loved ones and medical providers about end-of-life care, including the "What Matters to Me" workbook.

- https://tinyurl.com/ConversationCues - This resource "Conversation Cues" offers suggestions of how to discuss your loved one's health care preferences. Use this downloadable form to record their choices.

- aarp.org/caregiving - This website provides information about end-of-life planning and access to free advance directive forms by state.

- caringinfo.org/planning/advance-directives/creating-advance-directive/ - This article "Creating Your Advance Directive" provides an explanation of the various parts of the advance directive and what to consider when making these decisions.

- caringinfo.org/planning/advance-directives/storing-advance-directive/ - This article "Storing and Retrieving Your Advance Directive" provides information on how to safely store paper and digital directives as well as companies that offer these services.

- joincake.com - This website addresses end-of-life planning, including tools to create and store wills, advance directives, and many other resources.

- 5wishes.org - This organization provides a document, available digitally or in paper, to communicate personal, spiritual, medical, and legal decisions. These are valid in nearly all fifty states and also offer kits tailored to children, adolescents, and young adults.

- mydirectives.com - This website provides digital advance care planning and storage service for end-of-life documents. You may use your own forms or theirs.

- usacpr.com - The U.S. Advance Care Plan Registry registers and stores advance directives. This service provides additional amenities such as secured access to the health care community, wallet cards, and yearly update reminders.

- <u>polst.org/state-signature-requirements-pdf</u> - This website advises state-specific signature requirements for a Physician's Orders for Life Sustaining Treatment (POLST) to be valid. Each state has different requirements.

- <u>uswillregistry.org</u> - This online service securely records the existence and location of wills.

- <u>sidedrawer.com</u> - This digital vault service assures safety, accessibility, and security for all documents. Once documents are stored, register them with <u>uswillregistry.com</u>, which will give the location of stored documents to authorized representatives with photo I.D. and a copy of the death certificate.

- <u>ftc.gov/business-guidance/resources/complying-funeral-rule</u> - This website explains the Federal Trade Commission Funeral Rule, specific requirements in providing transparency, and full disclosure of prices of goods or services, as well as business practices with which funeral directors are required to comply.

- <u>gravematters.us</u> - This preview of Mark Harris's book *Grave Matters: A Journey Through The Modern Funeral Industry to a Natural Way of Burial* provides information on cremation, home funerals, and natural burials.

- <u>funerals.org</u> - The Funeral Consumers Alliance website offers a planning kit called "Before I Go You Should Know" as a digital download for a small fee.

Part 6: Navigating the Winding Path of Illness

- https://tinyurl.com/HighFiberFoods1 - Download a chart showing dietary fiber count for high fiber foods to help with constipation.

- https://tinyurl.com/CaloriesProtein - Download a list of foods to increase calories and a list to increase proteins, both associated with combating fatigue.

- dysphagiadietitian.com - This website offers resources developed by dysphagia dietitian Cat Ludwig RDN, LD to help manage chewing and swallowing difficulties related to nutrition and food texture.

Part 8: Understanding and Calming the Stress of This New Reality

- verywellhealth.com/breathing-techniques-8382890 - This article "Breathing Techniques Just About Anyone Can Try" explains ten breathing techniques used to reduce stress and ease anxiety.

- English Garden by Donahue Vanderhider - Access guided imagery.

- 3 Hours of Relaxing Music with Water Sounds Meditation on Vimeo - Access relaxing, meditative music.

- 3 Hours of Meditation Music for Deep Relaxation & Focus | Serene Soundscapes for Inner PeaceUltimate - Access meditation music.

- verywellmind.com/the-benefits-of-journaling-for-stress-management-3144611 - This article "Why You Should Keep a Stress Relief Journal" explains the benefits and strategies for journaling.

- nia.nih.gov/health/caregiving/caregiver-worksheets - The National Institute on Aging provides six different caregiver worksheets to download, print, and copy. They help coordinate care, identify hazards with a safety checklist, provide questions to ask before hiring a care provider, and questions to consider before moving an older or seriously ill adult into your home. There is also a worksheet to keep track of medications and supplements, and a checklist of important documents and other information to gather and store.

- aarp.org/caregiving/life-balance/info-2021/support-groups - This article "How to Find a Caregiver Support Group That's Right For You" provides information on the benefits of support groups for caregivers, what to expect, and how to find and join an online or in-person group.

- caringbridge.org/resources/caregiver-support-groups - This website provides tips for finding the right caregiver support group.

- https://tinyurl.com/CaregiversChecklist - This downloadable link provides the Caregivers Self-Evaluation Checklist.

Part 9: Options for End-of-Life Care

- inelda.org - The International End-of-Life Doula Association lists their membership of doulas by state to assist you in locating a death doula.

Part 11: The First Few Minutes in a World Without Your Loved One

- fda.gov/drugs/safe-disposal-medicines/disposal-unused-medicines -what-you-should-know - This website information is current as of October 2024. It includes specific instructions for the best ways to dispose of medication.

Part 12: In Memoriam

- funeralwise.com/funeral-planning/how-to-plan-a-funeral/ - This guide "Funeral Planning: A Complete Guide on How to Plan Your Funeral" helps you plan a service for your loved one or pre-plan for yourself. It considers all aspects of the process and ways to personalize the tribute.

- forevermissed.com - This website offers a wide array of templates for themes such as military, children, and other options for online memorials. The free plan offers background music. Visitors to the site may leave virtual flowers or lights.

- mykeeper.com - This website offers a free plan as well as a plus plan with a live virtual memorial, a geotag to the final resting place, and a scannable QR code to place on a headstone or marker to provide a link to a loved one's tribute page.

- everplans.com - This website provides a list of the ten most well-known online memorial websites.

Part 13: Personal Representative Responsibilities

- optoutprescreen.com- Opt out of prescreened offers permanently.

- dmachoice.org - Opt out of unsolicited mail for five years from organizations that use the Direct Marketing Association's Mail Preference Service.

- donotcall.gov - Register on the Do Not Call website to prevent solicitations. Certain organizations are exempt from this, including political organizations, charities, telephone surveyors, and companies with whom you have an established business relationship.

Acknowledgements

This book has provided many gifts, even before it has been read. Most of all: overflowing gratitude. From the beginning of this project, my world opened. I have met new friends and became closer with others. I understand how common it is to hide our fear of death and the pain we feel, knowing we all must face this ultimate experience. I have learned important lessons about humanity.

I am grateful to feel the support and love of my friends and family for this project, always respecting its priority in my life. I am honored that people shared their stories with me at the risk of their grief resurfacing. I am indebted to the many professionals in the medical and caregiving fields who gave their time and shared their insights to make this information as accurate and practical as possible. I took to heart the many people who told me they wished they had a book like this earlier in their lives, or that they needed it right now. I thank all who crossed my path on this journey. There are a few I would like to thank in particular.

First, my partner for fifty-six years and the very best part of my life for every one of them, my husband Greg. My rock. For the entire duration of this project, he rerouted much of his life. He took over every domestic chore and social obligation. He was my sounding board through fear and frustrations. He provided opinions, encouragement, and motivation when I felt stuck.

Brian John Skillen. My mentor, teacher, coach, and cheerleader—a consummate professional who consistently over-delivers. Founder of Publishing Hackers, award-winning author, international dance instructor, adventurer, and a really great guy. This book would never have even gotten past the idea stage if it were not for Brian and his team. He brought me from doubting I could do this, all the way through publication. He walked a computer-illiterate person (for the most part) through the writing process in weekly meetings, through thirty-nine steps of self-publishing, and marketing. He provided an excellent support team.

Whale Kangas, a kindred spirit and my content editor. She took a raw manuscript and did a lot of massaging to smooth it out. I was amazed that her edits were exactly what I was trying to convey—but better. Thank you, Whale.

Michael Brewer-Berres, Publishing Hackers' formatting editor extraordinaire (and my personal computer tutor!)—another talented person without whom this would not have happened. Thank you, Michael, for always being available for an emergency zoom meeting!

Tatiana Villa, cover designer. Thank you for guiding me in an entirely different direction. As everyone says, you are amazing.

Eathan Okura of Okura Law. Thank you for your time and patience, making a complicated subject a little less scary. Trusts and wills respect legal guidance.

Pam Clifton. Thank you for illustrating this. Your talents and friendship are always appreciated.

Kevin Hall. Thank you for your story, encouragement, and contacts!

Rev. David Dobler. Your instincts were right on. Thank you for your insights.

Bonnie Nichols, CHTP, Director of Organizational Experience, Central Peninsula Hospital. Thank you for being so generous with your time, program materials, and introductions to Frank Alioto and Dr. Warren.

Frank Alioto, MDIV. Thank you for sharing your experiences and support.

Dr. Angus Warren. Thank you for your insights into palliative care, and medical perspectives.

Bre. Founder of Rest With Radiance, President of Alaska End-of-Life Alliance, and end-of-life doula. Thank you for your time and expertise.

Sharon Bergstedt, RN, MSN, Director of Hospice and Palliative Care, Providence Hospice, Alaska. Thank you for generously sharing your time, expertise, and program materials.

Rena Queja, LCSW, SW Care Manager, Care Management Services, Providence Cancer Center. Thank you so much for such an interesting and inspiring interview.

Sarah Wilson, MPH, RD, CSO, LD. Thank you for your time, materials, and support for this project.

Andy Sorensen, my brother. "It's just you and me, kid". Thank you for supporting me and this project.

My son Jamie and his family- Thank you for your belief in me, it helped make this happen.

Cindy, Gloria, Cathy, Judy, and Donna, good friends and contributors to this book. You all are such inspirations to me. Thank you for your support, contributions to the book, and your friendship.

To my friend Kellene, the reason this book came to be. Life has only made us stronger. Thank you.

Glossary

Acupuncture: A traditional Chinese medical practice that involves inserting thin needles into specific points on the body to alleviate pain and treat various physical, mental, and emotional conditions.

Activities of Daily Living (ADL): Basic tasks essential for self-care, such as eating, dressing, toileting, and transferring (moving from bed to a chair).

Administrator: A type of personal representative appointed by the court if there is no will, if the will does not name an executor, or if the named executor is unable or unwilling to serve. The administrator's duties are similar to those of the executor, but they follow the state intestacy laws to distribute the estate.

Advance Directive: A legal document that consists of two main parts: the living will and the medical power of attorney. The living will specifies the types of medical treatments and life sustaining measures an individual wants or does not want. The medical power of attorney, also known as a health care proxy or durable power of attorney for health care, appoints a trusted person to make health care decisions on the individual's behalf, if the individual cannot communicate their decisions personally.

Against Medical Advice (AMA): A situation where a patient chooses to leave a health care facility or refuses treatment, despite being advised otherwise by a medical professional.

Anatomy Bequest Program: A program that allows individuals to donate their bodies after death for educational and research purposes, primarily to medical schools for the study of human anatomy.

Biofeedback: A technique that uses electronic monitoring devices to help individuals learn to control physiological processes, such as heart rate, muscle tension, and blood pressure, for improved health and performance.

Caseworkers: Health care professionals who assess patients' needs, provide counseling, and coordinate services to support patients' medical and emotional wellbeing during their hospital stay and after discharge.

Cardiopulmonary Resuscitation (CPR): A procedure that involves chest compressions and artificial ventilation to keep blood circulating and oxygen supplied in a person during cardiac arrest.

Cheyne-Stokes breathing: Breathing frequently observed during active dying, characterized by a cycle of slow, deep breaths followed by fast, shallow breathing, then a temporary stoppage of breath.

Death doula: A trained individual who provides non-medical support, comfort, and guidance to dying individuals and their families during the end-of-life process, helping with emotional, spiritual, and practical aspects of dying.

Durable Medical Equipment (DME): Medical equipment that is long-lasting and reusable, prescribed for use in a patient's home to aid in a better quality of life, such as wheelchairs, walkers, and oxygen tanks.

Do Not Resuscitate (DNR), Do Not Attempt Resuscitation (DNAR), Allow Natural Death (AND), No Code: Medical orders indicating that health care providers should not perform cardiopulmonary resuscitation if a patient's heart stops or they stop breathing.

Electronic Health Record (EHR): A digital version of a patient's medical history, maintained by health care providers, that includes all key administrative and clinical data relevant to the patient's care under a particular provider.

EHR integration: A process that connects patient data across different systems and facilities. It allows health care providers to access complete patient information in real-time, ensuring comprehensive and up-to-date records.

Ethical will (also known as a legacy letter): A document that contains expressions of a person's values, beliefs, life lessons, and personal reflections to share with loved ones, providing a legacy of non-material wealth.

Executor: A person appointed in a will to manage and distribute the estate of the deceased according to the terms of the will, ensuring that the decedent's wishes are carried out, and any debts and taxes are handled.

Financial durable power of attorney: A legal document that grants an individual, known as an agent, the authority to manage financial affairs on behalf of someone, even if that person is incapacitated.

Funeral home: A licensed facility that provides services related to the preparation, arrangement, and conduct of funerals, including the transporting and care of the deceased as well as support for their families.

Guided imagery: A relaxation technique that involves focusing on positive and calming images or scenarios, often led by a facilitator, to promote mental and emotional wellbeing.

Healing touch: A holistic energy therapy that uses gentle hand techniques to balance and support the body's energy system, promoting physical, mental, emotional, and spiritual wellbeing.

Home health aides: Trained health care workers who provide essential support to patients in their homes, assisting with activities of daily living (ADLs), such as bathing, dressing, and meal preparation, as well as monitoring health and providing companionship.

Hospice: A specialized type of care focused on providing comfort and support to terminally ill patients and their families, emphasizing quality of life, pain management, and emotional, spiritual, and psychological support. Typically provided in the patient's home or a hospice facility. Patients under hospice care have less than six months of life expectancy and have discontinued curative treatments.

Hospitalist: A hospital-based physician who specializes in the care of hospitalized patients. Hospitalists coordinate care with other specialists, provide comprehensive treatment, and manage patients throughout their stay.

Interdisciplinary Group (IDG): A team of health care professionals from various disciplines who collaborate to create and implement care plans for patients. This group often includes doctors, nurses, social workers, and other specialists working together to address the diverse needs of patients.

Incontinence: The inability to control the bladder or bowels, resulting in accidental leakage of urine or feces. It can vary in severity and may be caused by various medical conditions, age-related factors, or physical impairments.

Last will and testament: A legal document in which a person specifies how their assets and affairs should be managed and distributed after their death. It may also appoint guardians for minor children and name an executor.

Living will (Also see advance directive): A legal document that outlines a person's preferences for medical treatment in case they become unable to communicate or make medical decisions due to illness or incapacity. It guides health care providers, their medical power of attorney, or family members in making decisions about life sustaining treatments.

Licensed Clinical Social Worker (LCSW): A mental health professional who has completed the necessary education, training, and licensing requirements to provide counseling, therapy, and other social services. LCSWs often work in health care, schools, and private practice settings to support individuals and families.

Loving will: A document, and often a piece of memorabilia, that goes beyond medical and financial instructions, often including personal messages, memories, and wishes for loved ones. It conveys affection, values, and guidance to family and friends.

Medical power of attorney: A legal document that allows an individual to designate someone to make health care decisions on their behalf if they become unable to do so.

Mortuary: A facility where deceased individuals are prepared for burial or cremation. They often provide services such as embalming, arranging funerals, and handling the administrative aspects of death.

Oncologist: A medical doctor who specializes in diagnosis, treatment, and management of cancer. Oncologists may focus on specific types of cancer or treatment methods such as chemotherapy, radiation therapy, or surgical oncology.

Opiates: A class of drugs that refers to a naturally occurring substance from the opium poppy plant found in morphine and codeine. They belong to a broader category called opioids which includes natural opiates, synthetic, or semi-synthetic drugs. They act on opioid receptors in the brain to produce pain relief and other effects. Common opioids used today include codeine, morphine, hydrocodone, oxycodone, hydromorphone (Dilaudid), fentanyl, methadone, and buprenorphine. All are effective for pain relief and carry a risk of addiction.

Palliative care: A specialized form of medical care focused on providing relief from the symptoms, pain, and stress of serious illness. The goal of palliative care is to improve the quality of life for both the patient and their family, addressing physical, emotional, and spiritual needs. Palliative care is one of the core tenets of hospice care.

Personal representative (Also see administrator and executor): A broad term that encompasses both executors and administrators. They are responsible for managing and settling the estate of a deceased person.

Physician Orders for Life-Sustaining Treatment (POLST): A portable medical order, signed by the physician and patient, that dictates specific orders covering the types of treatments and interventions the patient may wish to receive or avoid. It is intended for individuals with serious illnesses or frailty.

Probate: The legal process of validating a deceased person's will and overseeing the distribution of their assets. This process includes verifying the authenticity of the will, appointing an executor or personal representative, paying debts and taxes, and distributing the remaining estate to the rightful beneficiaries.

Qi Gong: An ancient Chinese practice that combines physical movements, breathing techniques, and meditation to cultivate and balance the body's energy. It is believed to improve overall health, reduce stress, and enhance spiritual wellbeing.

Reiki: A Japanese healing technique based on the principle of channeling energy, known as "reiki" or "universal life force energy," through the practitioner's hands to promote physical, emotional, and spiritual healing.

Trust: A legal arrangement in which one party, known as the grantor, transfers assets to a trustee, who manages and holds those assets for the benefit of one or more beneficiaries. A trust can be revocable or irrevocable, providing various benefits such as asset protection, tax planning, and the orderly distribution of assets, according to the grantor's wishes. A revocable trust can be altered, amended, or revoked by the grantor at any time during their lifetime. An irrevocable trust cannot be changed, altered, or revoked by the grantor once it is established.

Tai Chi: An ancient Chinese martial art and exercise system that combines slow, deliberate movements, meditation, and breathing exercises. Tai Chi is practiced to improve physical health and balance, reduce stress, and enhance mental clarity.

Transcutaneous Electrical Nerve Stimulation (TENS): A therapy that uses low-voltage electrical currents delivered through electrodes placed on the skin to relieve pain. TENS disrupts the pain signals to the brain providing relief from muscle and joint pain as well as other types of acute or chronic pain.

Works Cited

Part 3: After the Words You Never Wanted to Hear

1. Dr. B. Miller and Shoshana Berger, *A Beginner's Guide to the End: Practical Advice for Living Life and Facing Death* (United States: Simon & Schuster, 2020).

Part 4: Perspectives from Different Stages of Life

1. "A Loving Will," "What to Do When Someone Dies," Central Peninsula Hospital (Soldotna, Alaska).

2. "How To Write An Ethical Will," EverPlans, https://www.everplans.com/articles/how-to-write-an-ethical-will.

Part 5: Decisions to Make, Communicate, and Record

1. Amanda Singleton, "Why All Adults Should Have A Living Will," What Is A Living Will and How Do You Make One, AARP, published August 2019, accessed 2024, http://www.aarp.org/caregiving/financial-legal/info-2019/what-is-a-living-will.html?msockid=00f675d3ee0164901cfc60f4ef2c6522.

2. *Conversations*, Central Peninsula Hospital (Soldotna, Alaska).

3. Amelia J. Barbus, "The Dying Patient's Bill of Rights," *American Journal of Nursing*, 75, no. 1, 1975, 99. https://www.joincake.com/blog/dying-persons-bill-of-rights/.

4. Funeral Costs and Pricing Checklist, Federal Trade Commission Consumer Advice, accessed December 29, 2024, https://consumer.ftc.gov/articles/funeral-costs-pricing-checklist.

5. David Sloan, "Most Americans are Choosing Cremation," 2022, https://theconversation.com/most-americans-today-are-choosing-cremation-heres-why-burials-are-becoming-less-common.

6. "Green Burial Defined," Green Burial Council, accessed December 29, 2024, https://www.greenburialcouncil.org/greenburialdefined.html.

Part 6: Navigating the Winding Path of Illness

1. "Nourish and Restore: A Nutrition Guide for Cancer," Providence Alaska Medical Center, (Anchorage, Alaska).

2. Jerlyn Jones, "10 Healthy Herbal Teas You Should Try," Healthline, accessed March 10, 2025, http://www.healthline.com/nutrition/10-herbal-teas.

3. Anne-Marie Rochester Keppel, *Death Nesting: The Heart-Centered Practices of a Death Doula* (Vermont: Inner Traditions/Bear, 2023).

4. "Nourish and Restore: A Nutrition Guide for Cancer," Providence Alaska Medical Center.

5. "Thrush: Treatment and Prevention Tips," Cleveland Clinic Health Essentials, 2024, https://health.clevelandclinic.org/thrush -the-white-stuff-growing-in-your-mouth-and-how-to-get-rid-of-it.

6. "Nourish and Restore: A Nutrition Guide for Cancer," Providence Alaska Medical Center.

7. "Delirium - Symptoms and causes," Mayo Clinic, 2022, https://www.mayoclinic.org/diseases-conditions/delirium/ symptoms-causes/syc-20371386.

Part 7: Hospitals: Making the Best of a Stay
1. Mark Harden, "What Are Hospitalists? And What Value Do They Bring to Health Care?," CU Anschutz Newsroom, 2024, https://news.cuanschutz.edu/department-of-medicine/hos pitalists-workload-burden.

Part 8: Understanding and Calming the Emotions of This New Reality
1. Michelle Pugle, "10 Useful Breathing Techniques to Try Anywhere," Verywell Health, 2023, https://www.verywellhealth.com /breathing-techniques-8382890.

2. Donald Collins, "The Power of Music to Reduce Stress," *Psych-Central*, August 2022, https://psychcentral.com/stress/the-power -of-music-to-reduce-stress.

3. Elizabeth Scott, "Why You Should Keep A Stress Relief Journal," *Very Well Mind*, October, 2023, https://www.verywellmind/the -benefits-of-journaling-for-stress-management-3144611).

4. "Caregiving in the United States 2020," AARP, https://doi.org/1 0.26419/ppi.00103.001.

5. "Caregiver Worksheets," National Institute on Aging, https://nia .nih.gov/health/caregiving.

6. Bruce Horovitz, "Caregiver Stress Takes a Toll on Mental Health," AARP, 2023, https://www.aarp.org/caregiving/health/info-2023 /report-caregiver-mental-health.html.

7. *A Caregiver's Guide to the Dying Process*, Hospice Foundation of America (Washington, DC: 1997).

8. "6 Simple (Yet Meaningful) Ways to Support a Caregiver," Caring-Bridge, 2024, https://www.caringbridge.org/resources/how-to-su pport-caregivers.

9. Marsha Mercer, "How to Find a Caregiver Support Group That's Right for You." *AARP*, March 2024, https://www.aarp.org/careg iving/life-balance/info-2021/support-groups.html.

Part 9: Options for End-of-Life Care

1. "Caregiving in the United States 2020," AARP, https://doi.org/1 0.26419/ppi.00103.001.

2. "Brief History of Palliative Care," *New England Journal of Medicine*, 2020.

3. Angela Morrow, "Four Levels of Hospice Care Defined by Medicare," Verywell Health, 2024, https://www.verywell-health.com/levels-of-hospice-care-1132297.

4. "Choices for Care with Advanced Cancer - NCI," National Cancer Institute, 2024, https://www.cancer.gov/about-cancer/advanced-cancer/care-choices.

5. *Providence Hospice Program* (Anchorage, Alaska).

6. Dr. B. Miller and Shoshana Berger, *A Beginner's Guide to the End: Practical Advice for Living Life and Facing Death.*

7. Christina Palmer, Patricia Pinto, and Katie E. Golden, "What Is a Death Doula, and When Should You Use One?," GoodRx, 2022, https://www.goodrx.com/health-topic/end-of-life/death-doula.

8. Anne-Marie Rochester Keppel, *Death Nesting: The Heart-Centered Practices of a Death Doula.*

9. "What Death Doulas Do:," accessed October 13, 2024, https://deathdoulas.com/whatdeathdoulasdo.

Part 10: The End in View

1. "Dehydration and End-of-life Care," Hospice of the North Coast, 2021, https://hospicenorthcoast.org/2021/08/04/dehydration-at-end-of-life-care/.

2. Anne-Marie Rochester Keppel, *Death Nesting: The Heart-Centered Practices of a Death Doula.*

3. Joseph Shega, "End-of-Life Timeline: Clinical Signs by Stage," VITAS Healthcare, 2023, https://www.vitas.com/for-healthcare-professionals/making-the-rounds/2020/march/signs-of-active-dying.

Part 11: The First Minutes in a World Without Your Loved One

1. Dr. B. Miller and Shoshana Berger, *A Beginner's Guide to the End: Practical Advice for Living Life and Facing Death.*

2. "What to Do When Someone Dies," Central Peninsula Hospital (Soldotna, Alaska).

3. "Green Burial Defined," Green Burial Council, accessed December 29, 2024, https://www.greenburialcouncil.org/greenburialdefined.html.

Part 12: In Memoriam

1. "Checklist: Plan a Funeral or Memorial Service," EverPlans, accessed January 07, 2025, https://www.everplans.com/articles/checklist-plan-a-funeral-or-memorial-service.

2. Dr. B. Miller and Shoshana Berger, *A Beginner's Guide to the End: Practical Advice for Living Life and Facing Death.*

3. "The Top 10 Online Memorial Websites," Everplans, accessed January 7, 2025, https://www.everplans.com/articles/the-top-10-online-memorial-websites.

Part 13: Personal Representative Responsibilities

1. "What Happens If There Is No Named Executor of the Estate?," Monk Law Firm, PLLC, published July 27, 2020, https://monklegal.com/what-happens-if-there-is-no-named-executor-of-an-estate/.

2. Sam Tetrault, "Who Needs Original Death Certificate After Someone Dies," Joincake.com, 2022, https://www.joincake.com/blog/who-needs-original-death-certificates/.

3. "What To Do When a Loved One Dies," United Way, https://www.unitedway.org/our-impact/financial-security/my-smart-money/immediate-needs/immediate-steps-to-take-when-a-loved.

4. "Agencies to notify when someone dies," USA.gov., accessed January 6, 2025, https://www.usa.gov/report-a-death.

5. "7 Common Scams to Look Out for When Someone Dies," everloved.com, https://everloved.com/articles/post-death-logistics/common-scams-to-look-out-for-when-someone-dies/.

Part 14: Grief and Bereavement

1. Alan D. Wolfelt, "The Mourner's Bill of Rights," Center for Loss & Life Transition, accessed October 13, 2024, https://www.centerforloss.com/wp-content/uploads/2016/02/MBR.pdf.

2. Elizabeth Kubler-Ross, *On Death and Dying* (New York, New York: Macmillan, 1969).

3. Karyn Arnold, "Facing Anxiety After the Loss of a Loved One," thegrieftoolbox.com, 2017, https://thegrieftoolbox.com/article/facing-anxiety-after-loss-loved-one.

4. Alejandra Vasquez, "How to Practice Self-Care While Grieving: Step-By-Step," Self-Care and Grief, 2022, joincake.com/blog/self-care-and-grief.

About the Author

P atty Rothwell, author of *How To Be Present At The End of Your Loved One's Journey*, places caring and compassion at the center of life. Her experiences being present at the end-of-life journeys for many people instilled a passion to help others through the painful event of losing a loved one through terminal illness. Patty attended final goodbyes with family, friends, caregivers, and people she had not met until trauma, tragedy, or the heartbreak of terminal illness entered their lives.

During much of her forty-three year career, Patty served as the Northern Regional Coordinator for Alaska Airlines and a responder for the Critical Incident Response Team, she was dispatched to assist survivors of catastrophic events of all sorts—from suicides of coworkers, to aircraft incidents and aviation disasters. Many times, she found the greatest pain came when loved ones realized their last chance to create a loving memory, a last touch, or say what needed to be said, was gone.

In Patty's first book, she shares insights and practical advice to manage the challenges we face being present with our dying loved ones. *How To Be Present At The End of Your Loved One's Journey* offers a compassionate guide to managing grief by helping people create meaningful final memories and providing comfort to readers and their loved ones in their end-of-life care.

Patty and her husband live in Alaska with their two golden retrievers, near their son and his family.

Follow Patty on Facebook as she shares more opportunities to learn how to be present and turn moments into memories.